The Photo Journalist
- A Memoir of Late Rajiv Kant

Rohit Kant

Printed in India

IndiePress

ISBN: 978-93-6045-548-4

First Printing, 2024

Indie Press

A division of Nasadiya Technologies Private Ltd.

Koramangala, Bengaluru

Karnataka-560029

http://indiepress.in/

Edited by Anagha Somanakoppa

Typeset by MAP Systems, Bengaluru

Book Cover designed by Rohit Kant

Publishing Consultant: Rechal Fernandes

Preface

My father, the late Rajiv Kant, began his journey in photojournalism in the mid-1970s. He was among the pioneering journalists in Bihar, working with the most advanced equipment available at the time. With my grandfather passing away at a young age, my father started working at just 16 years old.

Times were tough then, and my grandmother's only advice to him was, "Don't get arrested by the police." Despite the challenges, Mr. Arun Ranjan gave him his first break as a photojournalist at "Ravivaar." From there, he gradually earned opportunities to work directly and as a freelancer with all the major news houses and publications, spending most of his career with PTI.

My father left journalism in the mid-90s, disillusioned by the widespread malpractices in the press, many of which persist today. During the COVID lockdown, we had the chance to digitize his photographic treasures. We acquired a device from abroad that allowed us to convert many negatives to digital format. Although some negatives were damaged, the ones we salvaged were invaluable.

Sadly, my father passed away before completing this project, but it is an honour for me, as his son, to carry on this work. Though I may not do full justice to it, I am proud to share it. This collection has various themes and subjects, reflecting the socio-political atmosphere of Bihar from the 1970s to the mid-90s.

From Lalu Yadav's meteoric rise to Shatrughan Sinha's star power overshadowing his contemporaries, the book offers a journey through my father's lens. Each photograph is more than just an image; it is a narrative, a fragment of a larger story.

This book is written from my father's perspective and has no political affiliation. Thank you for joining me on this visual odyssey. May these images inspire you, bring you joy, and perhaps evoke some nostalgia for that era.

Contents

1. JP Movement

Lok Nayak Jay Prakash Narayan had started his movement against Indira Gandhi. The movement was spread nationwide and was the birth of a lot of non congress leaders, many still relevant today. It was not just a political movement, rather it was and till date the biggest movement by the people post independence.

Pix : Rajiv

Pix : Rajiv

Pix : Rajiv

2. Protest against Press Bill

In Bihar, on October 12, 1982, a Press Bill was hurriedly passed in the Legislative Assembly at midnight to curb journalists. Perhaps the then Chief Minister did this to show the central government. At that time, as today, there were supporters and opponents of the government. Those who supported the government began to face heavy opposition. Gradually, opposition to the Press Bill spread across the country, with journalists staging protests and demonstrations. There were no channels at that time. Political parties also started opposing vigorously, and the country witnessed widespread protests. After the journalists' decision, silent marches began at Bailey Road protest site, aiming to submit a memorandum to the Governor. I had already learned through IB that there would be a lathi charge today. I boarded a ladder-less bus in advance. As soon as the protest procession reached near the demonstration site, the lathi charge began. Upon receiving a wireless message, a police jeep was stationed near the police station. I jumped off the bus and ran, worried that my camera might get seized. Imagine all the editors of Patna, special correspondents of national newspapers, all journalists, and photographers were present, some even joined the protest.

3. Sampoorna Kranti Diwas

A large assembly was organized at Miller School in Patna on the occasion of the massive gathering of the 1990 JP Movement, marking the Sampoorna Kranti Day. Organized by Bhavesh Ji, the program was primarily attended by leaders such as Sachidananda Sinha, Lalu Prasad Yadav, Vashishth Narayan Singh, Shyam Rajak, Vikram Kuvar, Akhtar Hussain, and others. Bhavesh Ji presided over the meeting, and Lalu Prasad Yadav inaugurated the event.

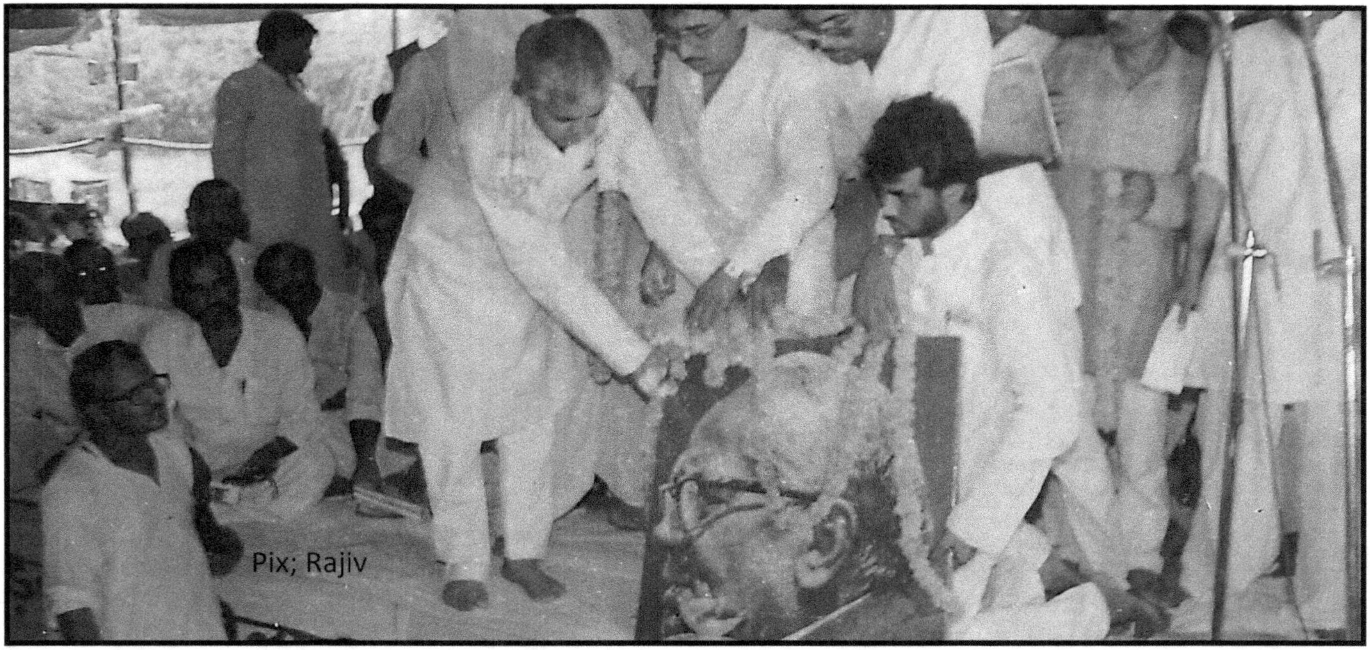

Pix; Rajiv

बिहार आन्दोलन के कर्मियों का
विशाल सम्मेलन
सम्पूर्ण क्रान्ति विद्यालय
Pix : Rajiv

बिहार आन्दोलन
संघर्षकर्मियों का
मिलर स्कूल मैदान, पटना
Pix : Rajiv

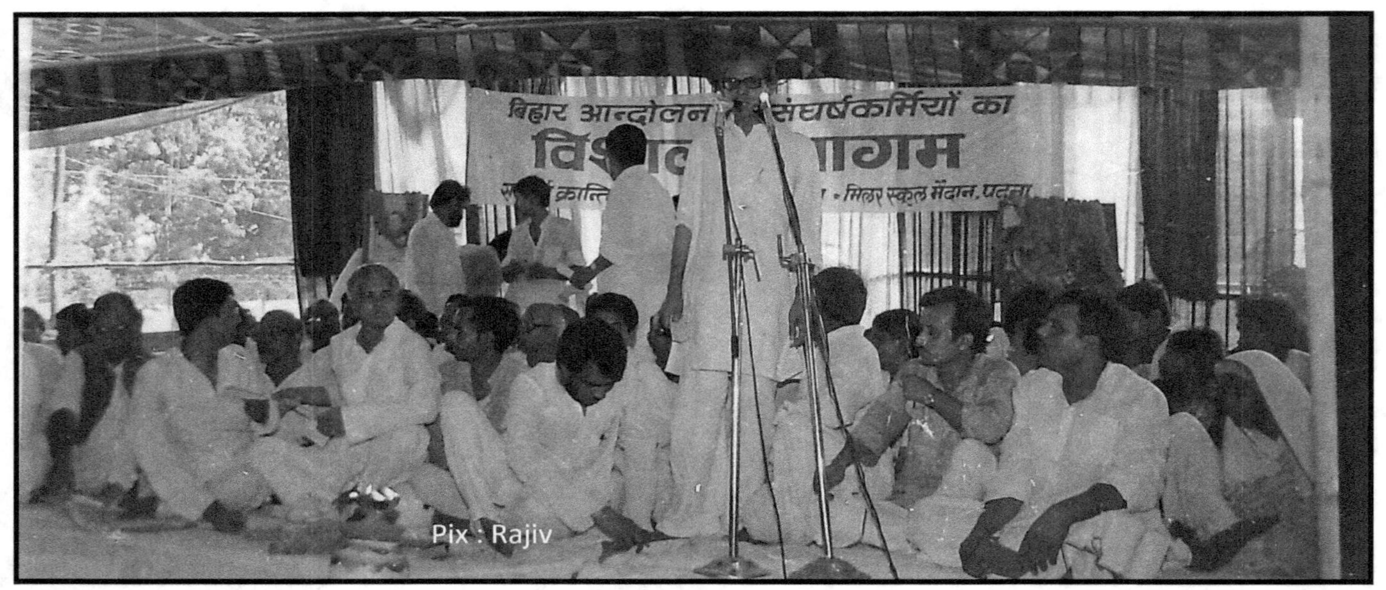

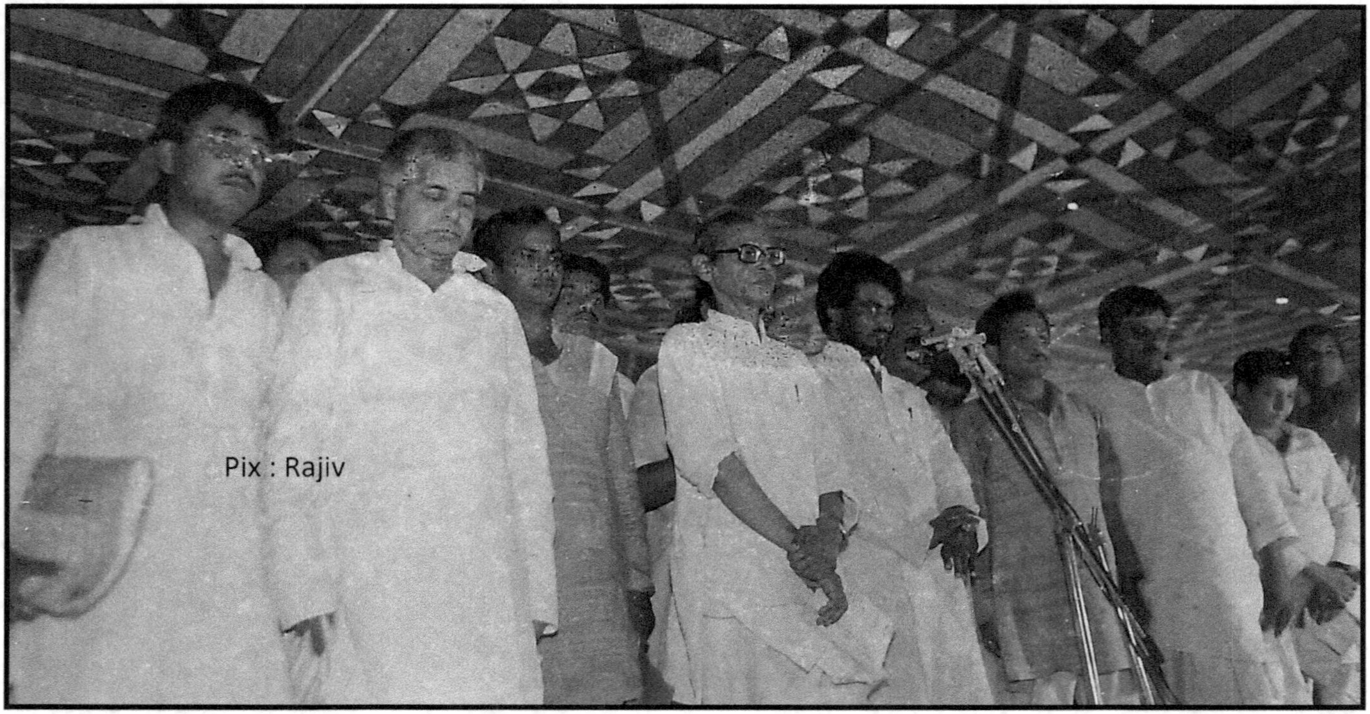
Pix : Rajiv

4. JP Jayanti and Poets Meet

In 1991, on the occasion of JP Jayanti, poets Satyanarayan and Gopi Ballabh Sahay from the JP Movement recited their poems. Gopi Ji performed his recitation at the Gandhi Museum, while poet Satyanarayan Ji recited his poem during the inauguration of JP's statue. From 1974 to 1977, these individuals held street gatherings at various locations as part of the JP Movement, and poetry recitation was an essential part of every gathering. Here are some photos from different places and of various people reciting poetry.

Pix : Rajiv

Pix : Rajiv

Pix : Rajiv

5. Meeting of the Opposition

The Rastriya Janata Party meeting was held at Jai Prakash Nagar in Kankarbagh. Hardly any big opposition leader was absent in this meeting. The National Conference held from 8 March to 11 March 1984 under the leadership of National President Chandrashekhar ji proved to be memorable.

The names of the prominent leaders involved in this meeting are as follows: Chandrashekhar ji, Chaudhary Devi Lal ji, Raj Narayan ji, Surendra Mohan, Mohan Dharia, Ramakrishna Hegde, Shahabuddin, Ramvilas Paswan, Kapildev Singh, Satyendra Narayan Singh, George Fernandes, Mohan Dharia, Murarka., Madhu Dandavate, Pramila Dandavate, Subramanian Swamy, Jabir Hussain, Subodh Kant Sahay, Sushma Swaraj and many other leaders.

क्रान्ति अब नारा है, आधी इतिहास हमारा है
ला पार्टी- द्वितीय राष्ट्रीय अधिवेशन
मार्च,

6. Bharat Pad Yatra

Bharat Pad Yatra, Chandrashekhar ji came to Patna via Sitab Diara. His foot journey passed through Vaishali and Hajipur and reached Bandarana. On the campus of Patna College, he was welcomed by the then President Anil Sharma. The then Chief Minister (Chhote Saheb) SN Sinha ji and Karpoori Thakur ji also welcomed him. Later there was a wreath laying program at JP residence. Ram Vilas Paswan ji also welcomed him in Hajipur.

यात्री (श्री चन्द्रशेखर) अभिनन्दन
(पटना विश्वविद्यालय)
आइये, हम आपका हार्दिक

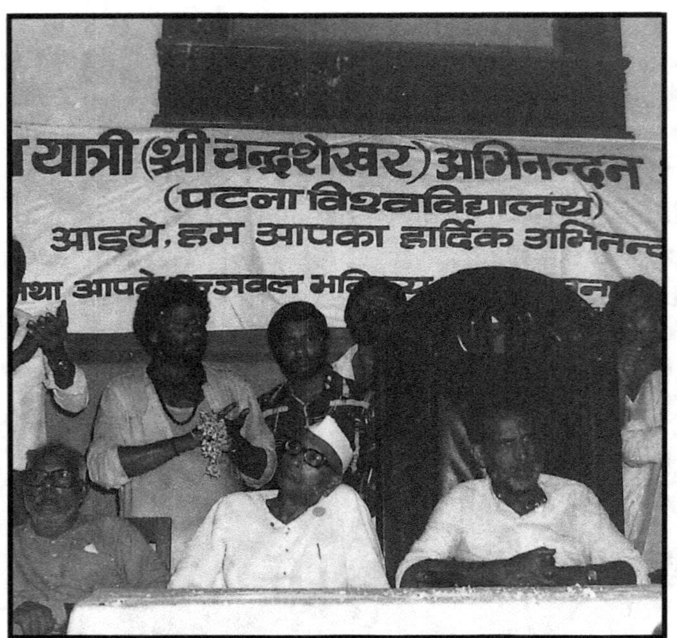

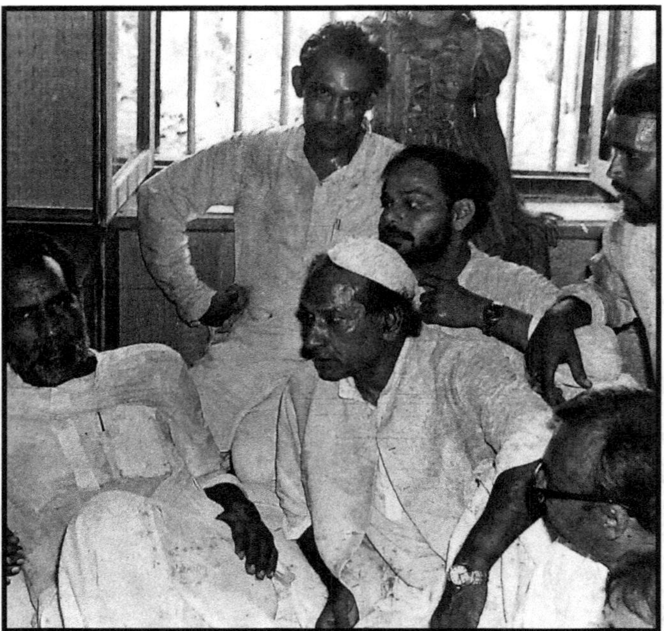

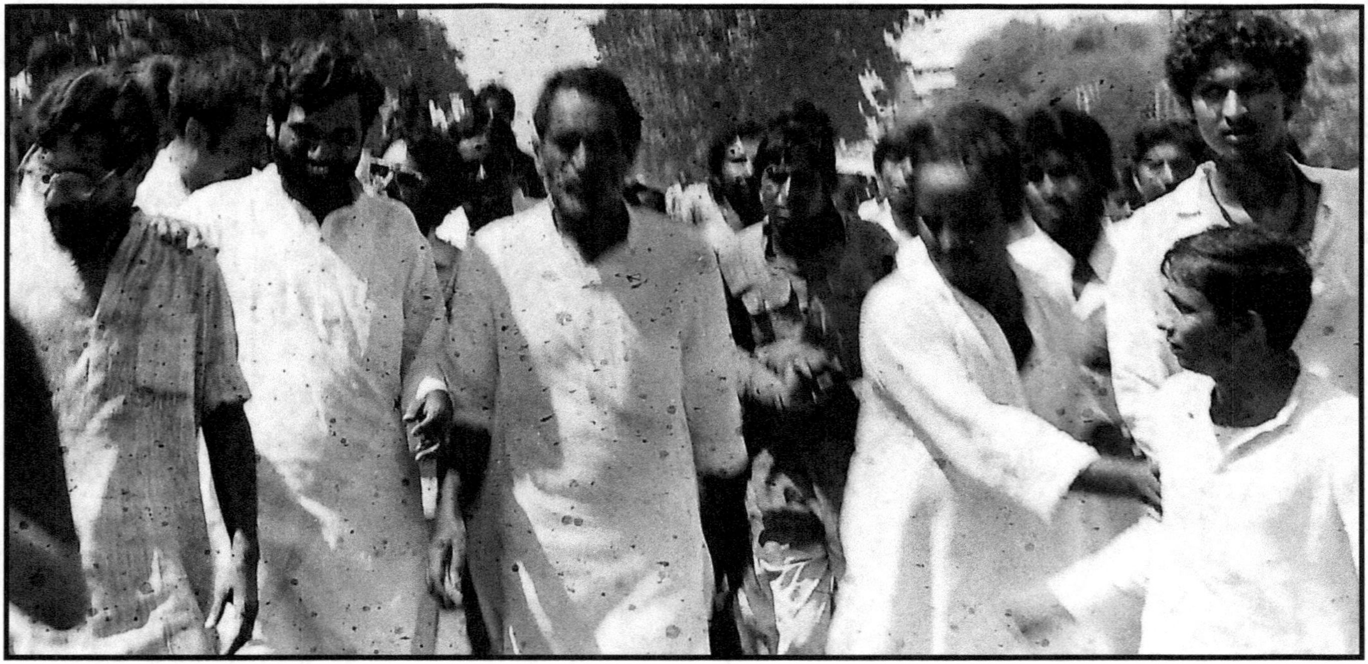

7. Chandrashekhar meeting the poor

In Bihar, once again the poor class was attacked by feudal lords. Chandrashekhar had reached Nonhi Nagma along with his associates Hukumdev Narayan Yadav and Subodh Kant Sahay. In the village he talked to the women and consoled them. Chandrashekhar ji was known for his simple nature and personality. He sat under a tree in the village and listened to the pain and suffering of the people.

8. Samajwadi and Janta Party Joint Rally

On June 19, 1992, a rally of Janata Party and Samajwadi Party was held at Gandhi Maidan. This meeting was inaugurated by Chandrashekhar ji, and the chief guest was Mulayam Singh Yadav ji, while Raghunath Jha presided. The ceremony was attended by Ram Bahadur Singh, Maneka Gandhi, Digvijay Singh, Lovely Singh, and Rajiv Pratap Singh at the airport, along with others.

Pix : Rajiv

Pix : Rajiv

Pix : Rajiv

9. Big Leaders gathered to meet Shiv Nandan Paswan

Upon hearing the news of Shiv Nandan Paswan Ji's deteriorating health, Chaudhary Devi Lal, Chaudhary Ajit Singh, Chandrashekhar Ji, V.P. Singh, along with others, went directly from the airport to his residence to offer their support. They assured him of any assistance he needed. Devi Lal also promptly provided financial help. At that time, the integrity of people was also evident. Gautam Sagar Rana and Akhtar Hussain were also present. Politics used to be different back then; upon learning about someone's situation, they would immediately go to meet them.

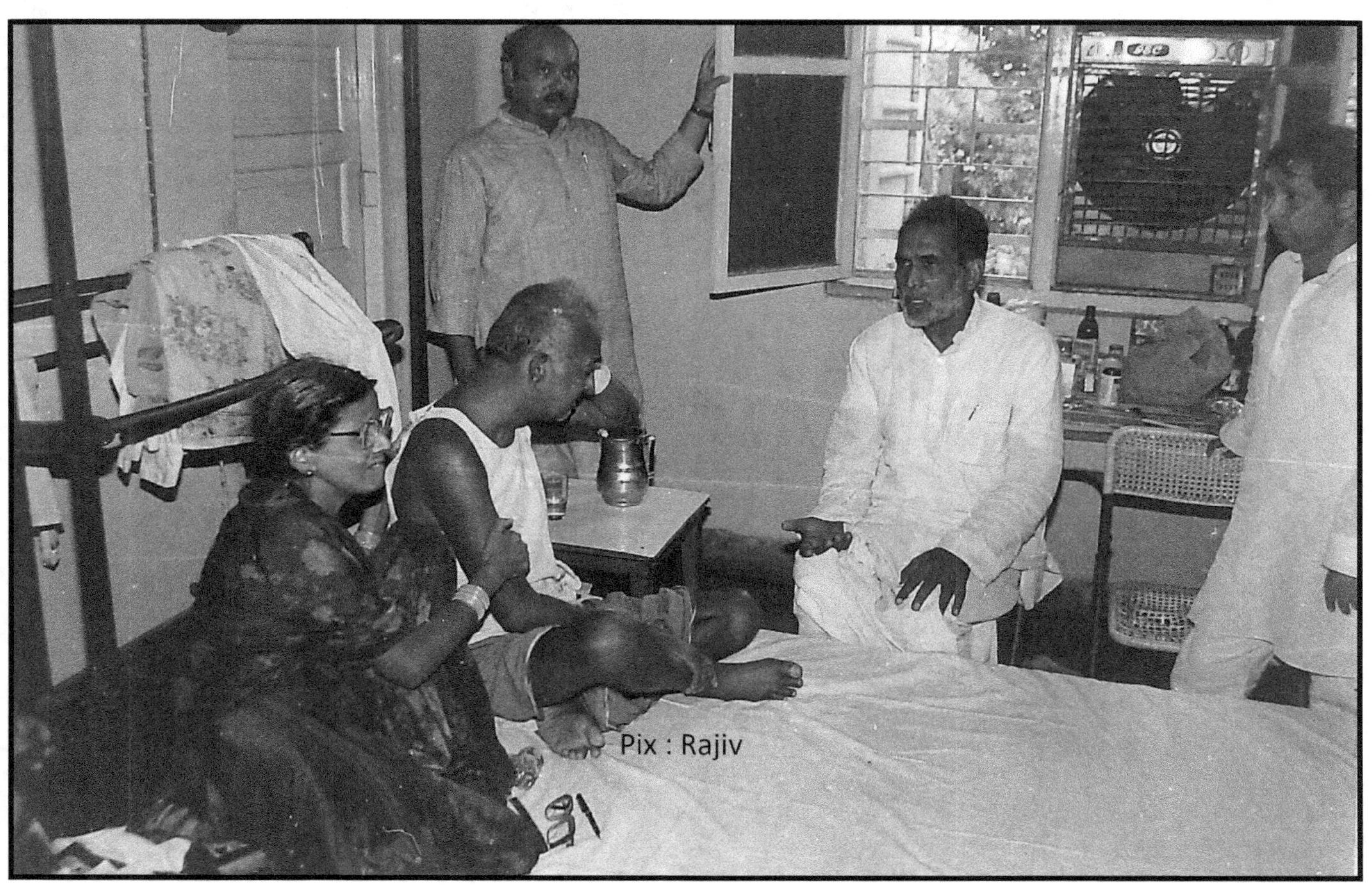

Pix : Rajiv

Pix : Rajiv

Pix : Rajiv

10. Launch of Nav Bihar Newspaper

Nav Bihar newspaper was launched in the 1990s, whose editor was Chandeshwar Vidyarthi. This new newspaper was started with full enthusiasm, and it was focused on the initiative of Satyendra Babu. Because of Satyendra Babu, the then Prime Minister Chandrashekhar ji inaugurated Nav Bihar. Chandrashekhar ji always did not change his approach towards recognition. Indian Nation editor Dinanath Jha, Satyendra Narayan Singh, Mithilesh Singh were also present on the stage.

Pix : Rajiv

Pix : Rajiv

Pix : Rajiv

11. Janata Party protesting against the Congress

Janata Party was protesting against the Congress government on various issues. There were two factions in the Janata Party: one faction was with Karpoori Thakur ji and the other with Tripurari Singh ji. However, when there was protest against the government, the whole of Patna became agitated. The procession used to reach the protest site on Bailey Road and a meeting was held there. According to tradition, the meeting was concluded by presenting a memorandum to the Governor. Public participation and support in such protests showed that people were dissatisfied with the policies and actions of the government.

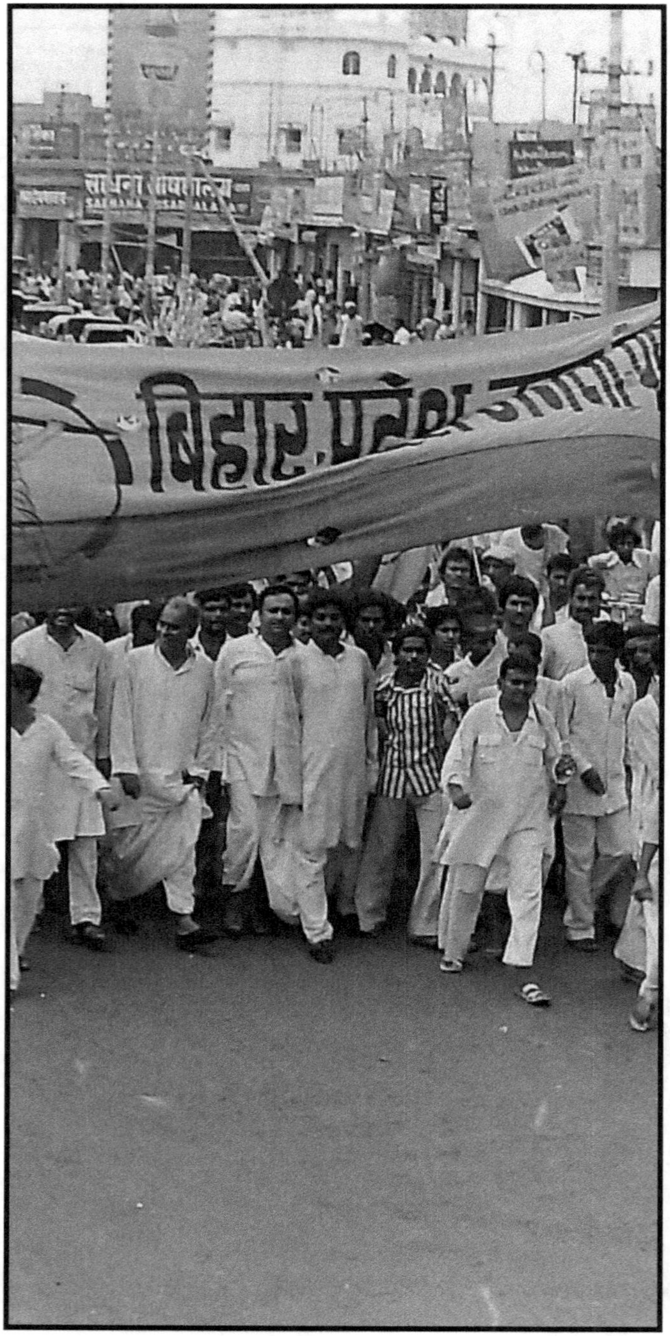
बिहार.प्रदेश

बिहार-प्रदेश-जनता पार्टी

LAMPS
KAJAL

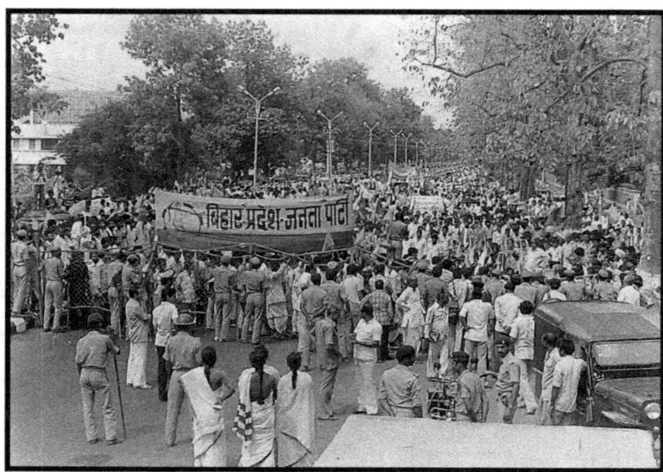

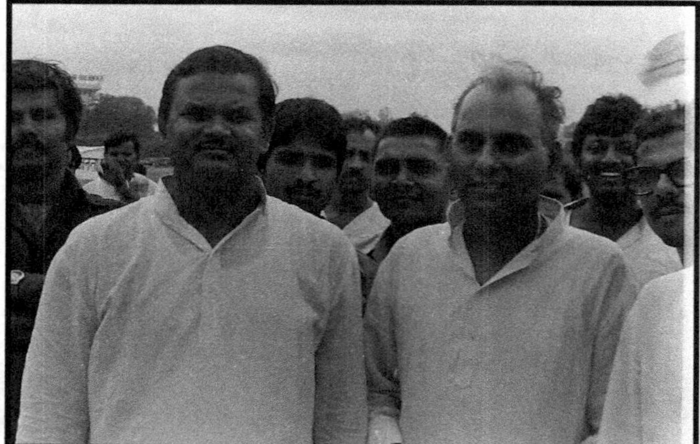

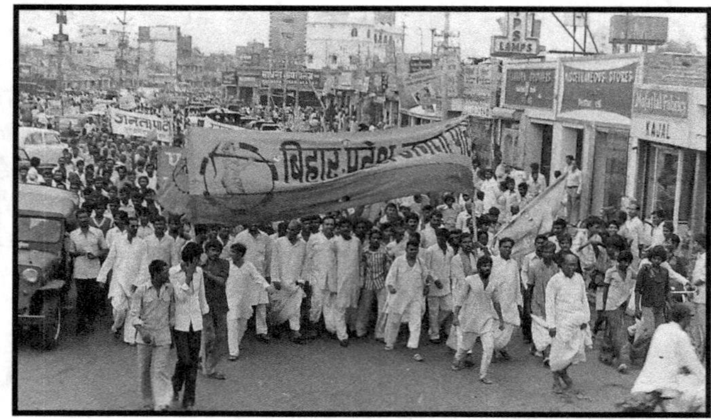

12. Iftar party organized by Karpoori Thakur

In 1986, the Iftar party organized by Karpoori Thakur ji included Chief Minister Bindeshwari Dubey ji, Mohd. Hidayatullah Khan and others. Hari Nath Mishra ji was also present in this picture. This party was a gateway to the Iftar of that time.

13. Anti Congress Meeting

In 1987, leaders from all opposition parties came together under the leadership of Karpuri Thakur to form a united front against the Congress. A rally was organized at Gandhi Maidan in Patna, where BJP's senior leader Rajmata Scindia, Chaudhary Devi Lal, Mulayam Singh Yadav, Hemvati Nandan Bahuguna, Ajit Singh, Kailashpati Mishra, Lalu Yadav, General S.K. Sinha, and many other leaders participated. Karpuri Thakur presided over the program.

14. March to Raj Bhawan by Karpuri Thakur

In 1988, Shivchandra Jha was the Speaker of the Legislative Assembly, and Karpuri Thakur was removed from his position in the opposition party under certain provisions. This caused a stir in the political corridors. At that time, all leaders stood with Karpuri ji. It was said that some party leaders were not with him. Karpuri Thakur led a march with legislators, starting from the Assembly to the Martyrs' Memorial and then to the Governor's House. During this march, senior legislators Lalu Prasad Yadav and Nitish Kumar also participated, standing shoulder to shoulder. Those legislators who were said not to be with him were also present at the Governor's House during this march.

Pix : Rajiv

Pix : Rajiv

Pix : Rajiv

Pix :   Rajiv

15. Meeting Indira Gandhi

On 05 September 1984, I had the opportunity to cover the program of Smt. Indira Gandhi, who was the Prime Minister at that time, two-three times. One of those press conferences was held at the State Hangar at Patna Airport. There was a call from PRD Director KC Mishra that Madam would speak in the State Hangar. Some select press members reached there and talks took place. I still remember that Indira ji's style of talking was different. She always spoke thoughtfully and her answers were always accurate and prompt.

**

Pix : Rajiv

16. V.P. Singh leaves Congress

Vishwanath Pratap Singh had left the post of Union Defence Minister and opened a front against Congress. First of all, he met Dr. Jagannath Mishra ji. A meeting was organized under the aegis of Congress Intellectual Forum. All the supporters of Dr. Jagannath Mishra ji had organized a meeting with Vishwanath Pratap Singh on 19 June 1987. Later he became Prime Minister from Janata Dal (United Front).

बिहार काँग्रेस बुद्विजीवी मंच
मुख्यवक्ता- श्री विश्वनाथ प्रताप सिंह
(पूर्व रक्षा मंत्री, भारत सरकार)
दिनांक :- १६ जून ८७ पटना

17. Lalu Yadav selected as Janta Dal Leader

On March 7, 1990, Lalu Prasad Yadav, leader of the Janata Dal, was elected. There were three candidates for the leadership position: Ram Sundar Das, Raghunath Jha, and Lalu Prasad Yadav. The election process proceeded under the supervision of a decisive committee that included Mulayam Singh Yadav, Sharad Yadav, Ajit Singh, and George Sahab. Nitish Kumar oversaw Lalu ji's election process to ensure that every vote was accurately counted. Raghunath Jha was positioned to split Ram Sundar Das's vote, a strategy widely discussed in political circles. Had Jha not been there, Das would have become the Chief Minister.

Pix : rajiv

Pix : Rajiv

Pix : Rajiv

18. President Venkatraman visit in Patna

On 11 December 1990, the then President His Excellency Ramaswami Venkatraman ji came to Patna on a two-day visit. I accompanied him on his tour. He was welcomed at the Patna airport by then Chief Minister Lalu Prasad Yadav, Governor Mohammad Yunus Salim, and Patna Mayor Shyam Babu Yadav. Along with other programmes, he also went to JP residence and garlanded the statue of JP.

When Venkatraman ji started going to garland the statue, Patna police personnel stopped him from going up. Immediately the President's Press Advisor Bhatnagar Saheb requested the President to wait for a minute and immediately called me and took me upstairs. Then the wreath laying was done and then I could take photos. In a photo, Lalu ji is seen introducing Vashishtha Narayan Singh ji. Later I also received a letter of appreciation from Rashtrapati Bhavan.

19. Lalu Yadav's Village in Gopalganj

In the 1990s, when Lalu Ji was the Chief Minister, we visited his village, Phulwaria in Gopalganj. Abdul Ghafoor was also with us. At that time, we went to his village. The villagers were very happy that Lalu bhaiya had become the Chief Minister. His brothers and family members came to meet him. Nephews, nieces, and many others came to pay their respects. Lalu Ji was overseeing the construction of his new house there. After spending some time and giving instructions, Lalu returned.

Pix : Rajiv

Pix : Rajiv

Pix : Rajiv

Pix : Rajiv

Pix : Rajiv

20. Lalu Prasad Yadav's Birthday

In 1990, after Lalu Ji became the Chief Minister, his first birthday was celebrated with great enthusiasm. At that time, Radha Nandan Jha lived in the adjacent house and was the first to arrive to congratulate him. He was accompanied by Rajo Singh, Ilyas Hussain, Jayprakash Yadav, and several other dignitaries. Gradually, more people arrived and the cake-cutting continued. Lalu Ji, along with his sons Tej Pratap and Tejaswi, cut the cake, marking the celebration of his birthday.

Pix : Rajiv

Pix : Rajiv

Pix : Rajiv

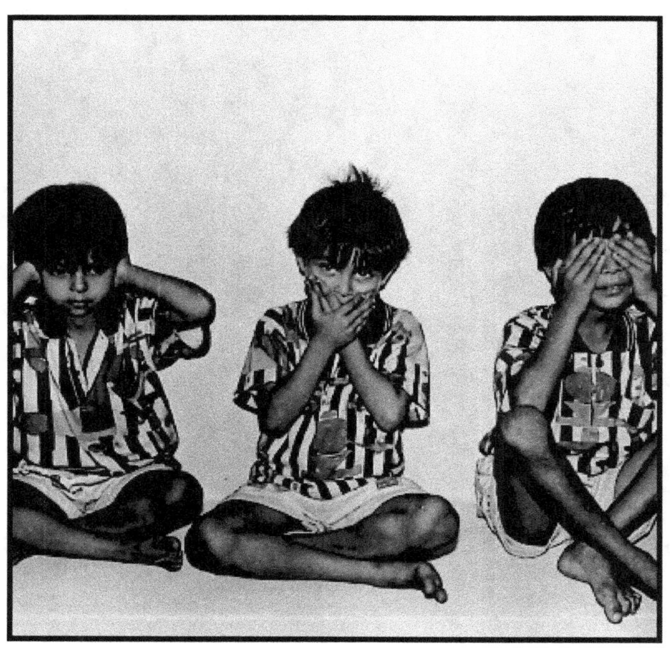

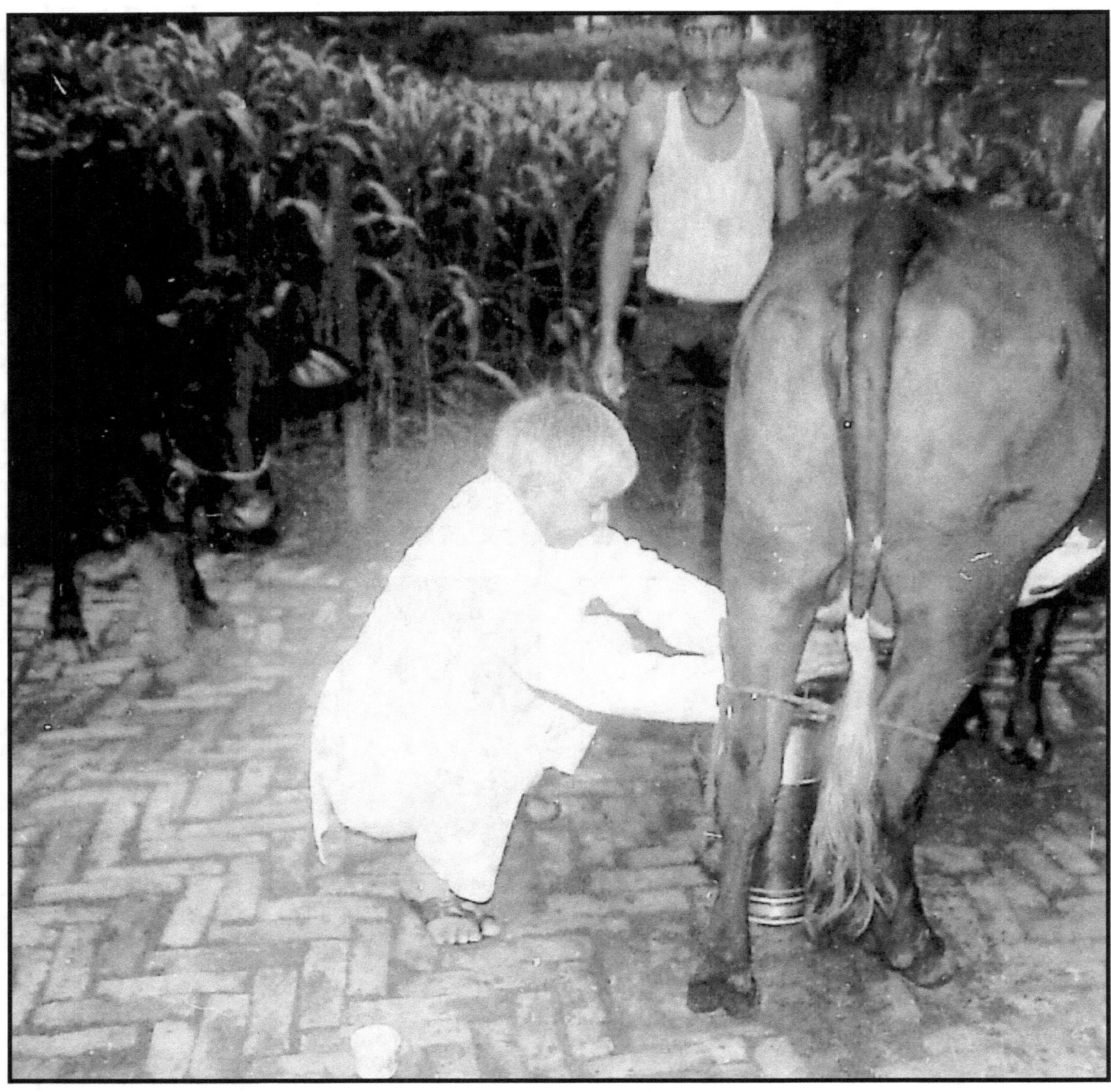

21. When Lalu and Nitish were together

There was a by-election in Bihar in the 1990s. At that time both Lalu ji and Nitish ji used to attend all the programs together. If Lalu ji had reached earlier, he would have waited.

Pix : Rajiv
Pix : Rajiv

22. Election Campaigns in 1990 and 1995

There was an unforgettable scene during the election campaign of 1990–1995. Wandering from the helicopter, getting down and talking to people, asking about the Chief Minister of Bihar, the answer used to be "Lalua hai," and his reply was "Hum hi Lalu hai." Listening to Lalu ji's speech, sitting on a buffalo and attending the meeting, all these were unique experiences. There were some interesting photos, which included Nitish ji, Ramkripal ji and others.

Pix : Rajiv

Pix : Rajiv

Pix : Rajiv

Pix : Rajiv

23. Indra Kumar Gujral

In 1992, Lalu Prasad Yadav nominated Inder Kumar Gujral for Rajya Sabha member from the Janata Dal during his tenure as Chief Minister. At that time both Nitish Kumar and Lalu Prasad Yadav were together. Nitish ji had helped in filing nomination papers. Nitish Kumar along with other MLAs while filing nomination and Inder Kumar Gujral ji with Lalu ji celebrating the victory, later he became the Prime Minister.

स्वागत वाराणशी

24. Garib Rally

Lalu Prasad Yadav's biggest rally, the Garib Rally, was held at the historic Gandhi Maidan. Many big leaders including VP Singh, SR Bombay, Jyoti Basu ji and Sharad Yadav participated in this rally. Patna was packed during the rally and the scene was amazing. The whole of Patna was filled with crowd.

Pix: Rajiv

25. Kurmi Chetna Manch

In 1994, some internal discord started between Lalu Prasad Yadav and Nitish Kumar. The result was that after the Garib Rally, the Kurmi Rally organized by Kurmi Chetna Manch was also very successful. Gradually people started coming in favour of Nitish Kumar. Many prominent people from Ravi Rai to Vinay Katiyar had participated in this rally.

x : Rajiv

26. Bihar Bachao Andolan – Subodh Kant Sahay

This story is from 1989. During the Congress government, there was a lot of political upheaval in Bihar. Around that time, Shatrughan Sinha made a significant impact in Bihar politics. He would often visit Bihar two or three times a month. Under the Bihar Bachao Andolan led by Subodh Kant Sahay, Shatrughan Sinha was brought into the fold. Several meetings were held to plan a state-wide campaign in Bihar.

बिहार बचाओ अभियान
राज्य प्रतिनिधी सम्मेलन
विद्यापति भवन, पटना - 18 सितम्बर 1989
Pix : Rajiv
राज्य प्रतिनिधी सम्मेलन
विद्यापति भवन, पटना - 18 सितम्बर 1989

Subsequently, Shatrughan Sinha formed the Fans Association in Bihar, which included Anang Bhushan Varma "Bablu," Brajesh Raman, Sanjay Mayukh, Prem Ranjan Patel, Sanjay Tiger, Sanjay Sahay, and many other young men. On Shatrughan Sinha's birthday on December 9, a blood donation camp was organized near JP Murti Gandhi Maidan, where Anang Bhushan "Bablu," along with all his companions, donated blood. Shailendra Nath Srivastava inaugurated the event. Navin Kishore Sinha, Ashwani Chaube, Rajiv Ranjan Prasad, Shyam Rajak, and friends of Shatrughan Sinha such as Pradeep Gupta, Praveen Sinha, and Dr. S.K. Sinha, led the blood donation drive. Later, Shatrughan Sinha joined the Bhartiya Janata Party (BJP).

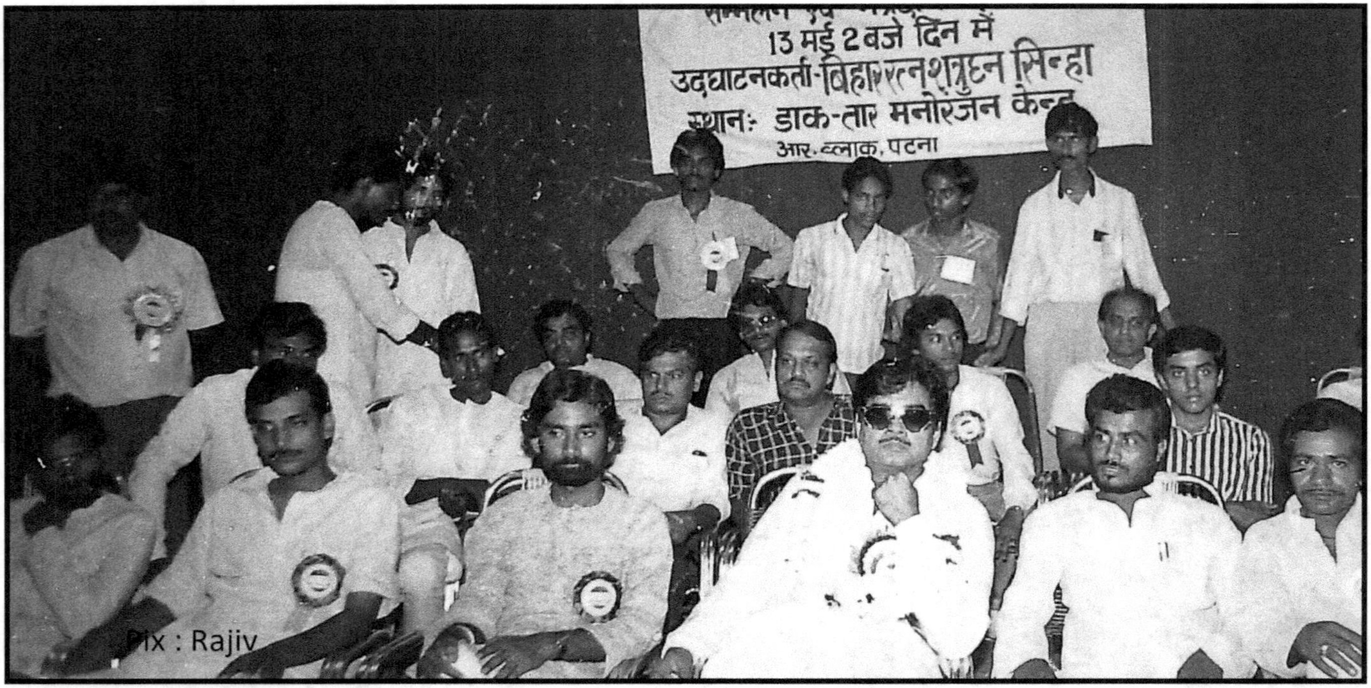
13 मई 2 बजे दिन में
उदघाटनकर्ता-बिहाररत्नशत्रुघ्न सिन्हा
स्थानः डाक-तार मनोरंजन
आर.ब्लाक, पटना
Pix : Rajiv

सम्मेलन एवं नेत्रदान शिविर
13 मई 2 बजे दिन में
उदघाटनकर्ता-बिहाररत्नशत्रुघ्न सिन्हा
स्थानः डाक-तार मनोरंजन केन्द्र
आर.ब्लाक, पटना
Pix : Rajiv

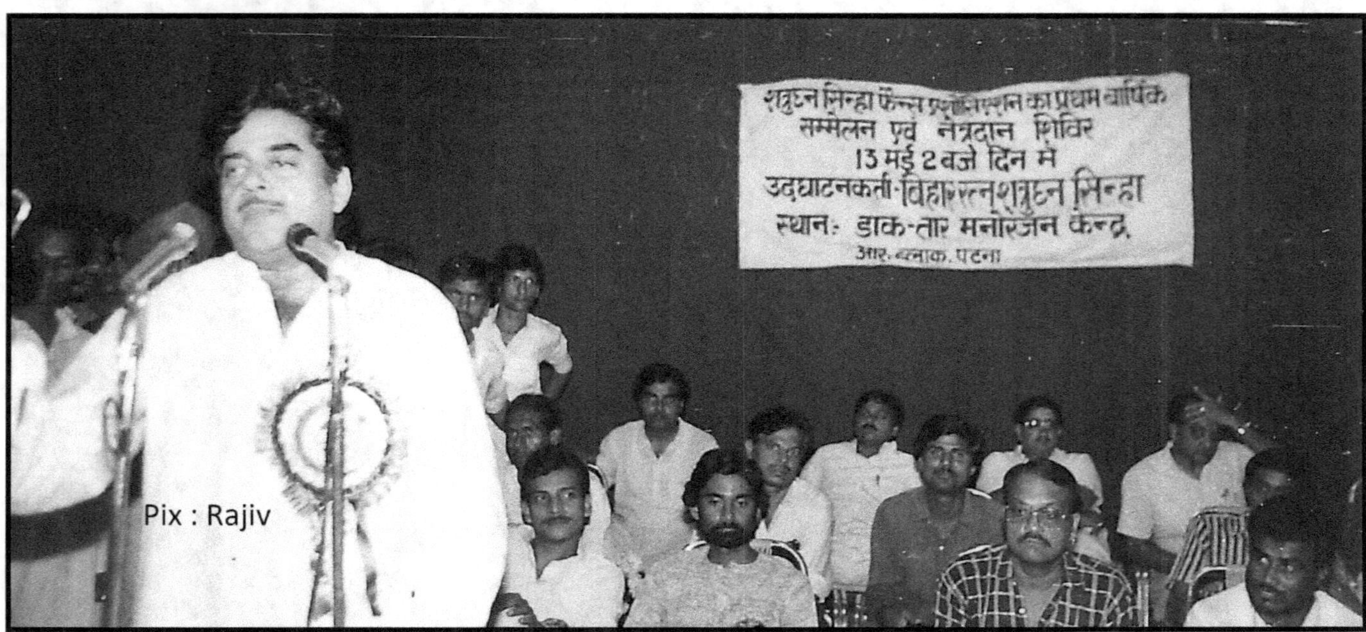

Pix :Rajiv

27. Shatrughan Sinha in a dhaba

Film actor Shatrughan Sinha and some journalist friends, such as Krishna Murari, Lok Pal Sethi, and Dr. Shatrughan Kishore, talking while sitting in a dhaba on their way to Darbhanga in September 1988 after the earthquake. This was the time of Shatrughan Sinha ji's beginning of politics in Bihar.

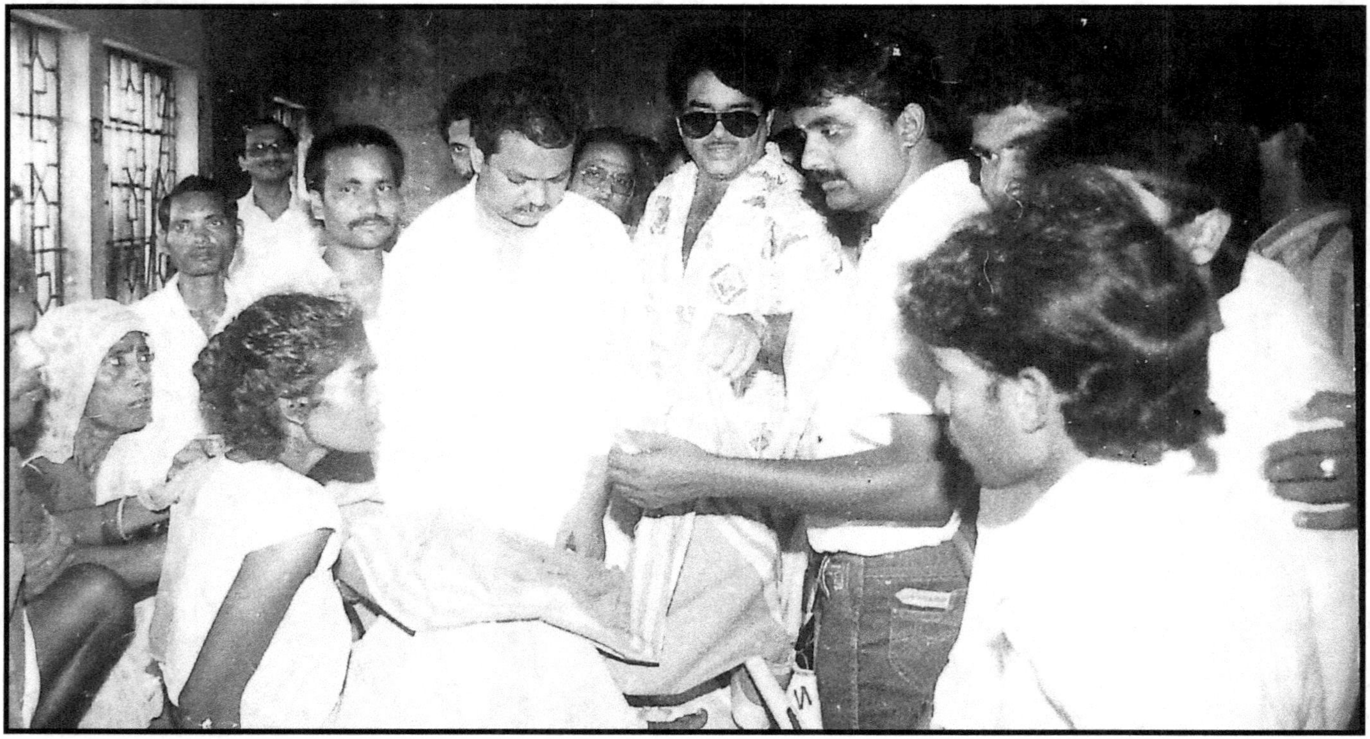

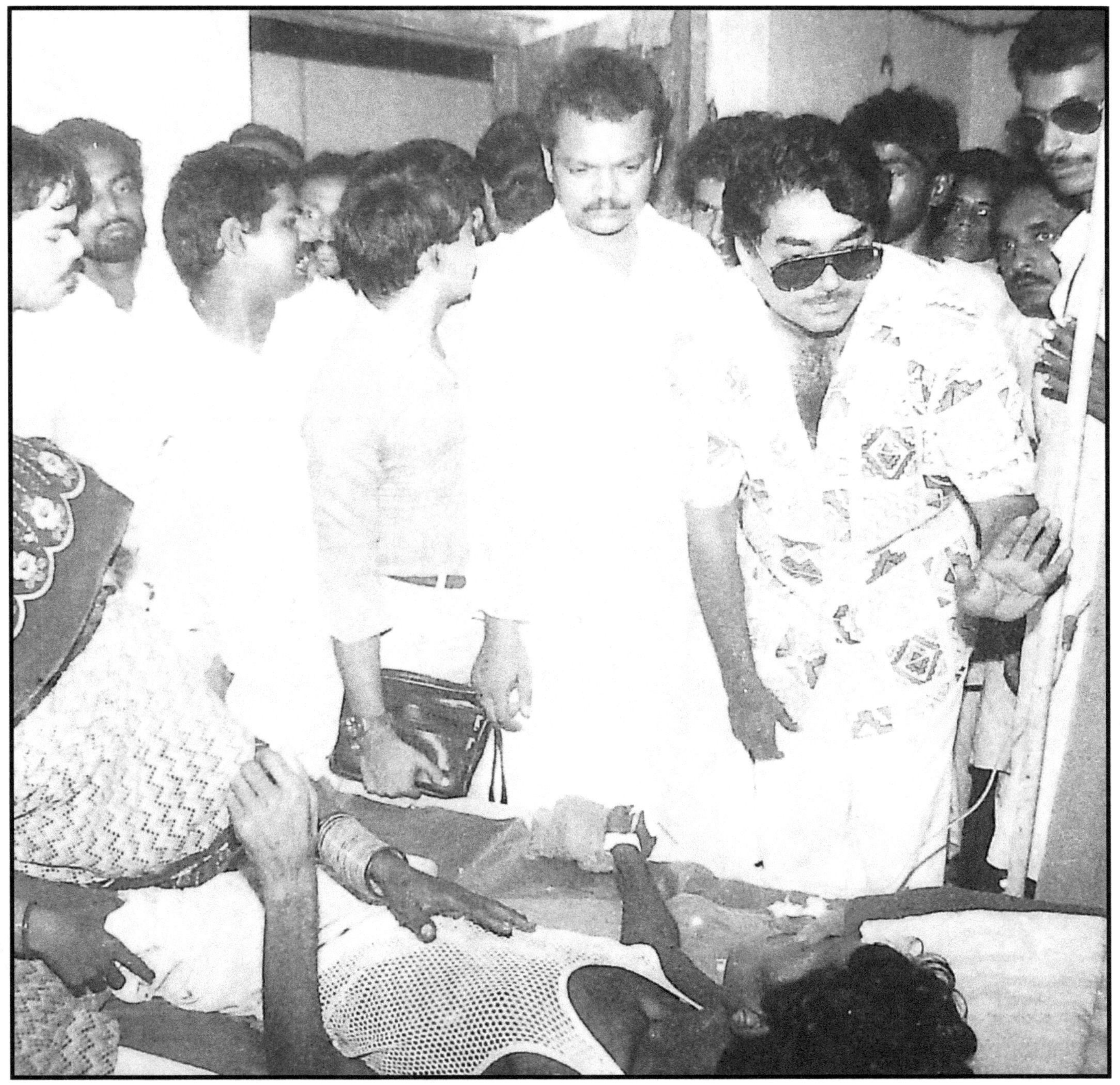

28. Shatrughan Sinha in Bhartiya Janata Party

In the 1990s, when Shatrughan Sinha joined the BJP, he conducted an election campaign for the Lok Sabha elections alongside Kailashpati Mishra. After arriving directly from Patna Airport to the election field, a grand rally was held at Patna's Gandhi Maidan with Atal Bihari Vajpayee. While Vajpayee was delivering his speech and Shatrughan Sinha arrived on stage, chants of "Bihari Babu Zindabad" filled the air. Vajpayee also praised Shatrughan Sinha. These photographs from that time, taken at Bikram, Danapur, and Gandhi Maidan, which include Kailashpati Mishra, Shailendra Nath Srivastava, Ravi Shankar, Ganga Babu, and others.

Pix : Rajiv

Pix : Rajiv

Pix : Rajiv

Pix : Rajiv

Pix : Rajiv
Pix : Rajiv

Pix : Rajiv

29. Bhartiya Janata Party's strong rallies in Bihar

In the 1990s, programs of BJP's top leaders were held in Gandhi Maidan. Programs featured Kalyan Singh, along with Thakur Prasad Ji, Kailashpati Mishra Ji, Sushil Modi, and Tara Kant Jha Ji. In another program, Atal Bihari Vajpayee Ji, Murli Manohar Joshi Ji, Kailashpati Mishra Ji, Uma Bharti were present. While, Shatrughan Sinha Ji, Shailendra Nath Srivastava Ji, and Ravi Shankar Ji were also on stage.

Pix : Rajiv

30. Star Campaigner Shatrughan Sinha

The then chief campaigner of BJP and film actor Shatrughan Sinha ji had addressed Bihar Sharif and Nawada on 22-02-1994 during his two-day tour. This incident was probably part of the BJP Kisan Morcha. BJP President Ashutosh ji, present His Excellency Governor Ganga Babu, Chandrani ji, Brajesh Raman, Prem Ranjan Patel and other BJP leaders also participated in this program. In Bihar Sharif, Chandrani ji had welcomed Shatrughan Sinha ji with shawl and khukhra.

31. Shatrughan Sinha Fans Association

In the 90s, Shatrughan Sinha ji was associated with the Save Bihar movement. At that time some youth had formed Shatrughan Sinha Fans Association. Bhushan Babul, Brajesh Raman, Prem Ranjan Patel, Sanjay Prakash Mayukh, Sanjay Tiger, Rakesh Ranjan Bablu, Manoj Srivastava and others were involved in it. Later some of these people became MLAs, like Prem Ranjan Patel, Sanjay Mayukh and Sanjay Tiger. Brajesh Raman became vice president of BJP, Manoj Srivastava became producer at Doordarshan, and Rakesh Ranjan Bablu became PR head at Tata Power.

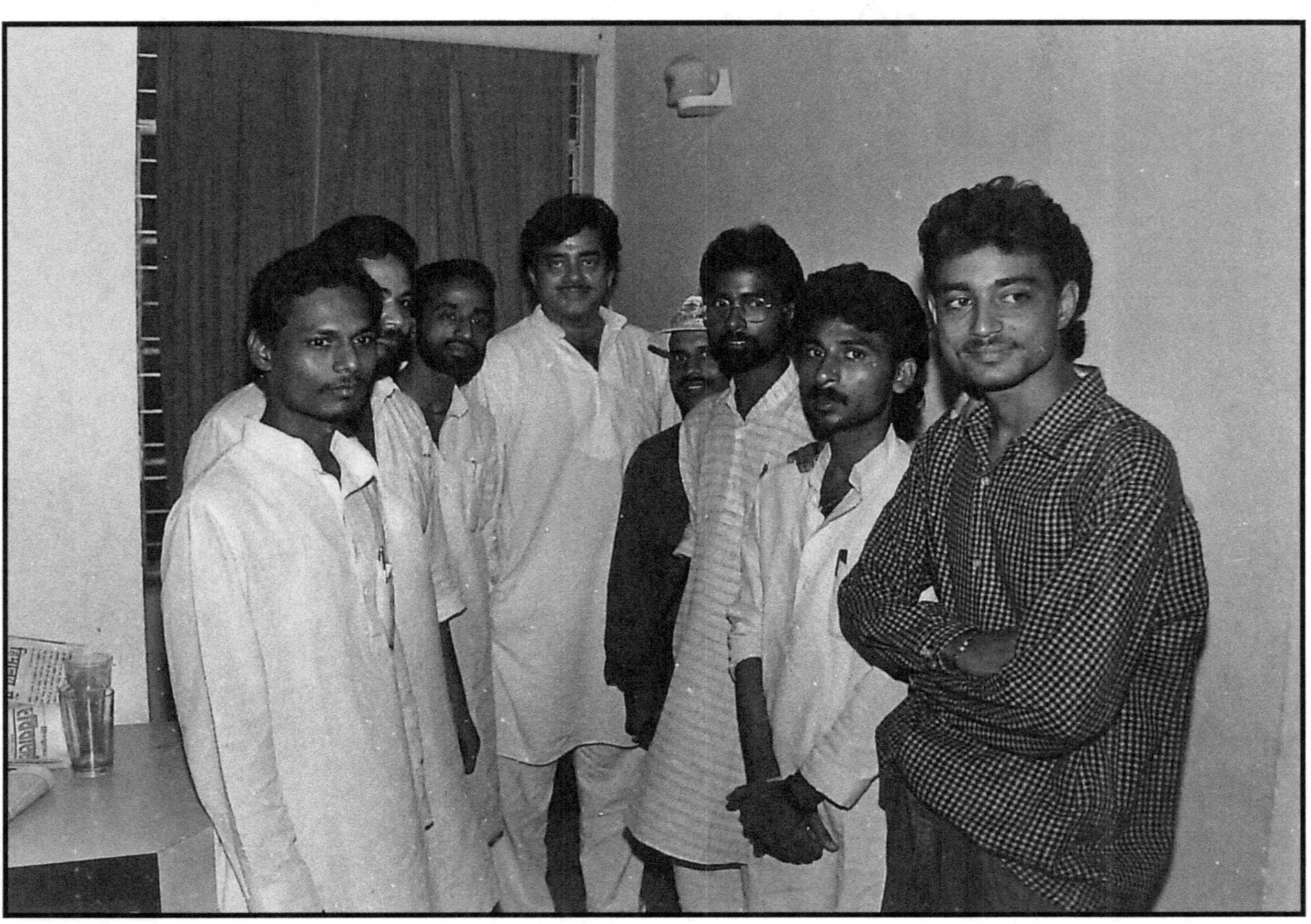

32. Lala and Gwala

All India Kayasth Festival was held in 1992, which was presided over by N.N. Sahay ji did it. The chief guest was Shatrughan Sinha ji and the inauguration was done by Lalu Prasad ji. On this occasion, everyone had expressed their views, but Lalu Prasad ji's style of presenting his views was different. He said, "Lala Gawala Ek Hi Na Hota Hai," on which there was a wave of laughter in the entire pandal.

अखिल भारतीय कायस्थ महासभा
का
१०८ वाँ राष्ट्रीय अधिवेशन, पटना

अखिल भारतीय कायस्थ
का
१०८ वाँ अधिवेशन

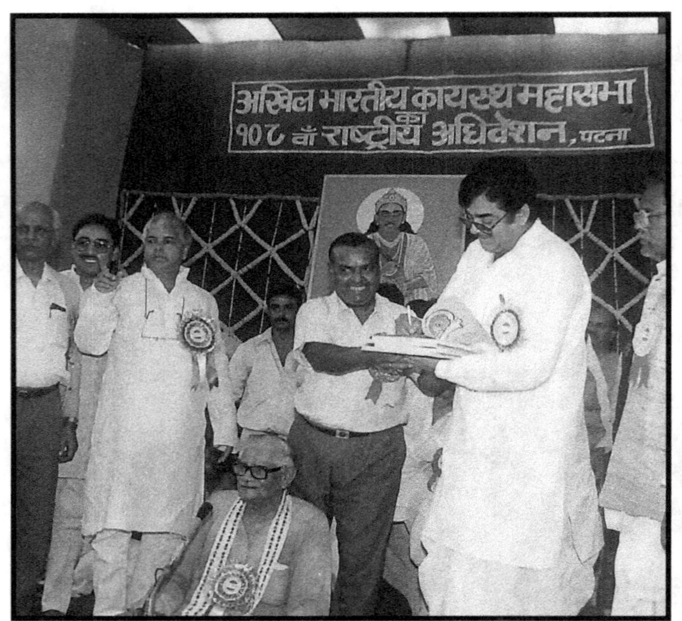

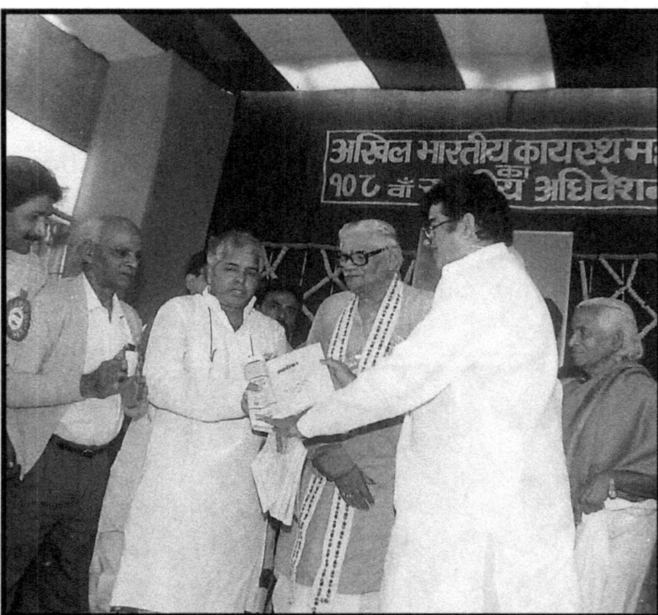

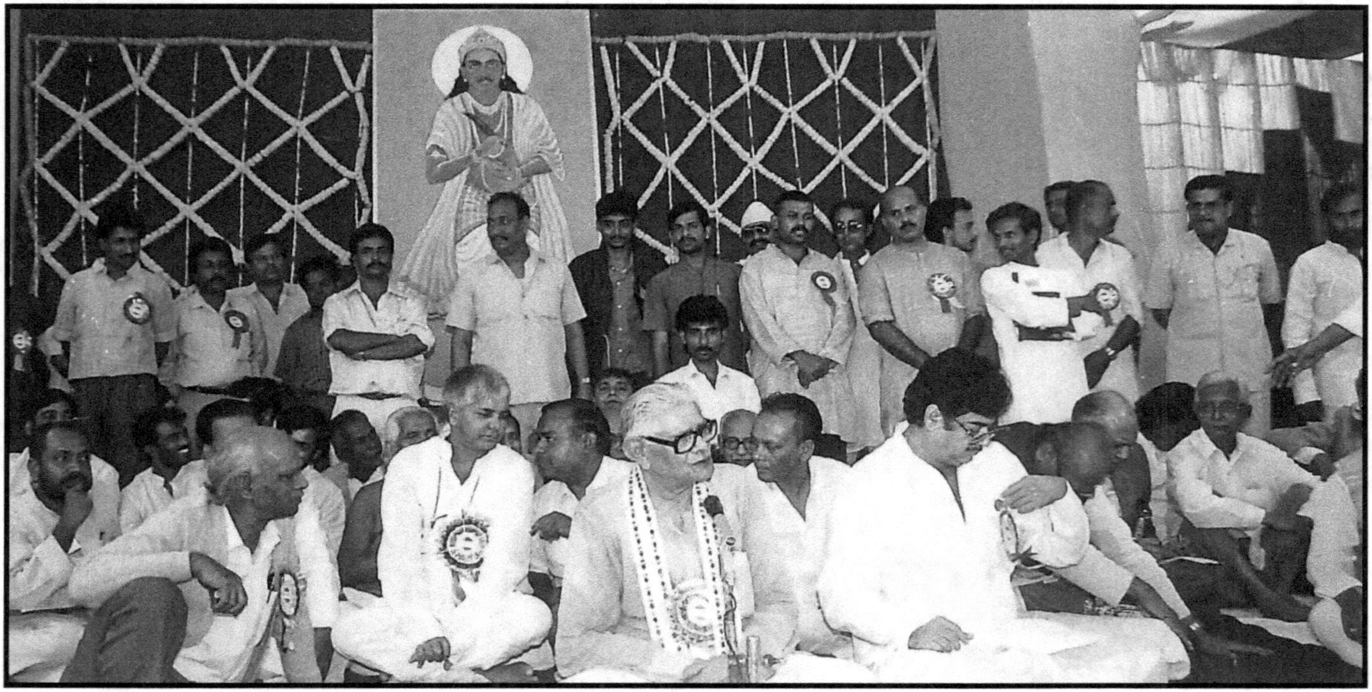

कायस्थ महासभा
राष्ट्रीय अधिवेशन, पटना

33. Somnath to Ayodhya Rath Yatra

Senior BJP leader Lal Krishna Advani's Rath Yatra from Ayodhya to Somnath took place in 1990, in which it had to pass through Bihar. At that time Lalu Prasad Yadav ji was the Chief Minister. Before arresting Advani ji, the Chief Minister took permission from Prime Minister VP Singh ji. Subsequently, at 4 a.m. on 23 October 1990, when everyone was sleeping, he was secretly arrested and sent in a state government helicopter to the Masanjore Guest House in Dumka under tight security. The journalists accompanying Advani ji in the Rath Yatra also did not know about his arrest and no photographs could be taken. Later, Advani ji's daughter Pratibha Advani and her son-in-law were sent to Dumka by state government plane to meet them, where security was tight.

सोमनाथ से अयोध्या

34. Protest against Rath Yatra

During Advani ji's Rath Yatra, protests were being organized by various organizations in Patna. Advani ji was staying in Morya Hotel. During this period, litterateurs, artists, Vahini and other organizations protested. There were also clashes with BJP workers during these protests.

हम सब बहनें एक रहेंगी।
स्त्री-मुक्ति संघर्ष वाहिनी

कोई मजहब या पहचान
पहले हम सब हैं इन्सान
आडवाणी की साम्प्रदायिक रथ यात्रा का बहिष्कार करें
ایڈوانی کی تعصبانہ رتھ یاترا کی مخالفت کریں
- इन्सानी एकता मुहिम

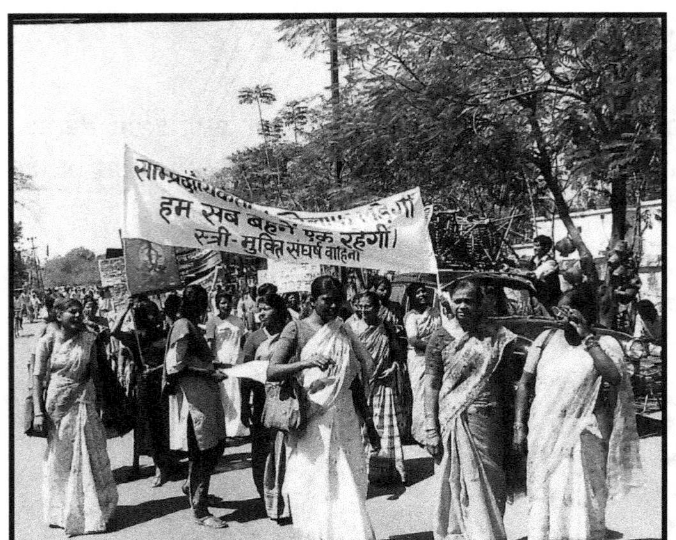

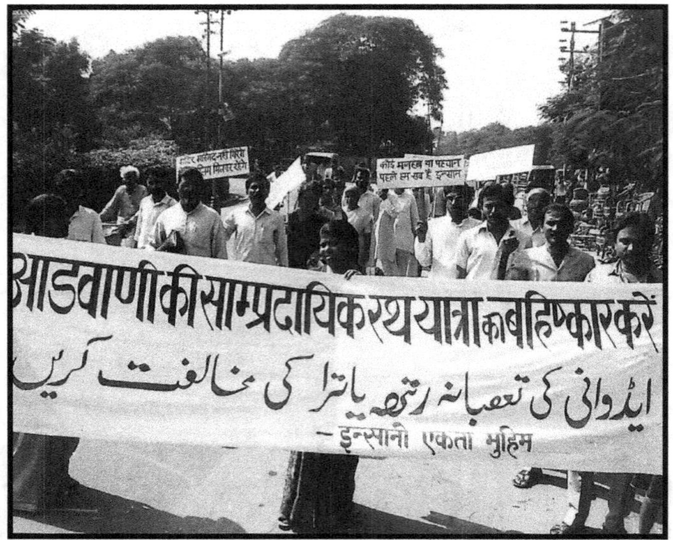

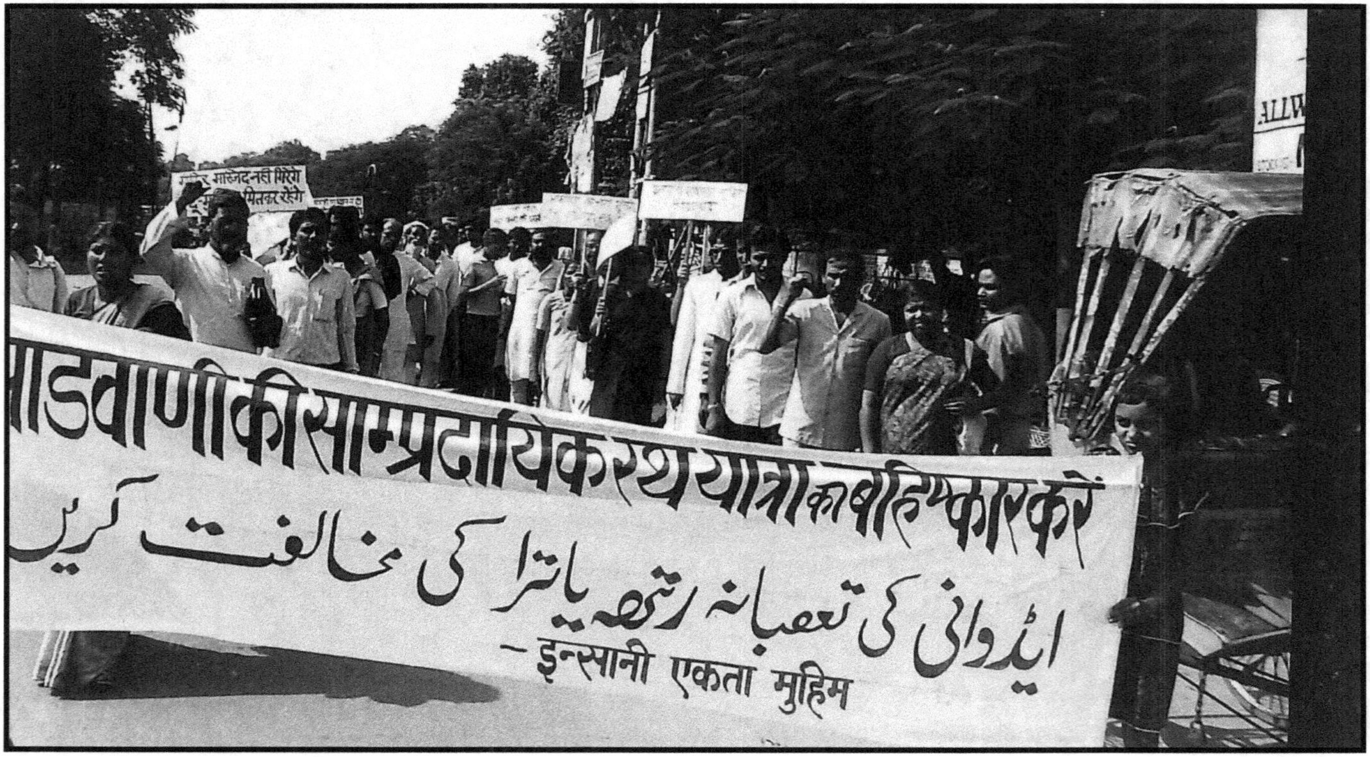
आडवाणी की साम्प्रदायिक रथ यात्रा का बहिष्कार करें
ایڈوانی کی تعصبانہ رتھ یاترا کی مخالفت کریں
- इन्सानी एकता मुहिम

मंदिर मस्जिद नहीं गिरेंगे
हिन्दू मुस्लिम एक रहेंगे

सद्भावना जुलूस
सद्भाव समिति
पटना-८०००१

35. Youth Congress in Bihar

When Rajiv Gandhi became the General Secretary, there was a stir in Bihar's Youth Congress, and Sitaram Kesari's blessings were upon the youth leaders of Bihar. In 1989, Tarik Anwar became the National Youth President. There were youth leaders in Bihar at that time, including some legislators and active workers. Some photographs from that time remind us of Prime Minister Rajiv Gandhi, Bhagwat Jha Azad, Tarik Anwar, Sharad Jain, Sarfaraz Ahmed, Ashwani Sharma, Shashi Kant Tiwari, Shyam Sundar Singh Dheeraj, Satdev Singh, Karuneshwar Singh, Shankar Yadav, Pandey ji, and others who were pillars of this youth movement.

Pix : Rajiv

Pix : Rajiv

Pix : Rajiv

Pix : Rajiv

Pix ; Rajiv

Pix : Rajiv

Pix : Rajiv

Pix : Rajiv

36. Rajiv Gandhi giving Interview

Z Ahmed, news editor of Doordarshan Patna, had interviewed Rajiv Gandhi. He had decided to do this interview on the way while returning from Teeskhora, but on the request of Ahmed Saheb, Rajiv Gandhiji talked to him. At this time Dr. Jagannath Mishra ji was also sitting with him.

राज
उद्घाटनकर्ता = श्री राजीव गाँधी,

37. Rajiv Gandhi visits to meet Dalits

In the 90s in Bihar, after the killing of Harijans and Dalits in Teeskhora (Patna Rural), former Prime Minister Rajiv Gandhi went to Teeskhora village, where he spoke with IPF workers. On the other hand he met Ram Sundar Das and Himanshu ji's family. Whenever any kind of incident took place in Bihar, opposition leaders used to reach places and demand action, like Karpoori Thakur, Ram Sundar Das and other leaders had done.

Pix : Rajiv

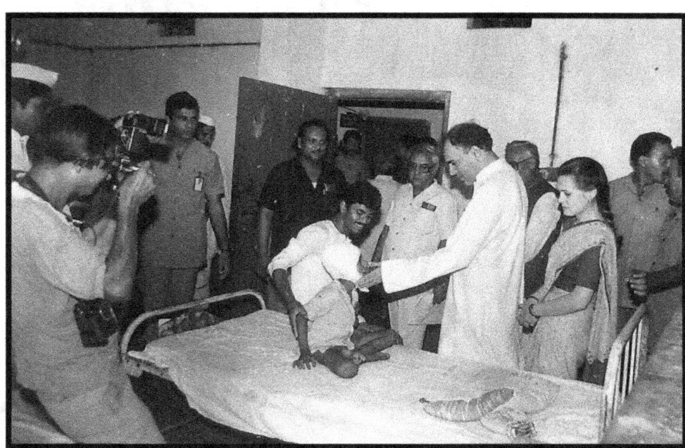

38. CITU National Conference in Patna

The national conference of CITU was held on 3 March 1994 at Gandhi Maidan, Patna. This conference was inaugurated by West Bengal Chief Minister Jyoti Basu. Let it be known that Jyoti Basu ji was the Chief Minister of India for the longest period. After the conference, a worker rally was also organized at Gandhi Maidan, in which Jyoti Basu ji addressed the workers. Other senior leaders of CPI(M) were also present at the event, including Harkishan Singh Surjit, Ganesh Shankar Vidyarthi, Sitaram Yechury and other senior leaders. The event was very important and was attended by workers from all over the country.

TU
DIAN TRADE UNIONS
CONFERENCE

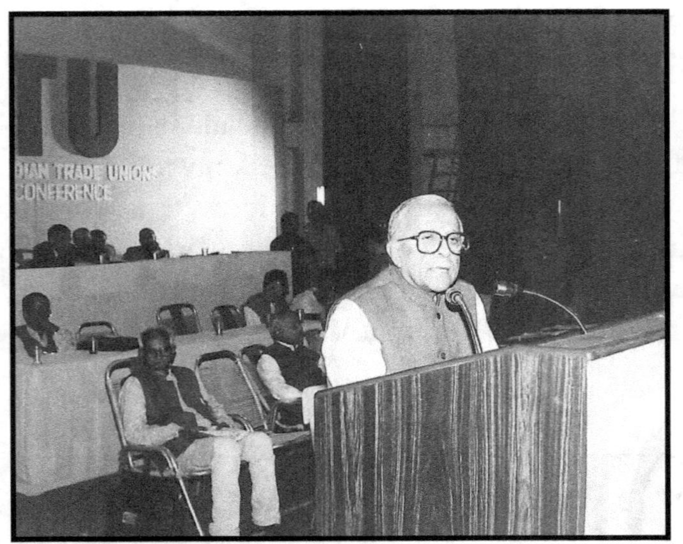

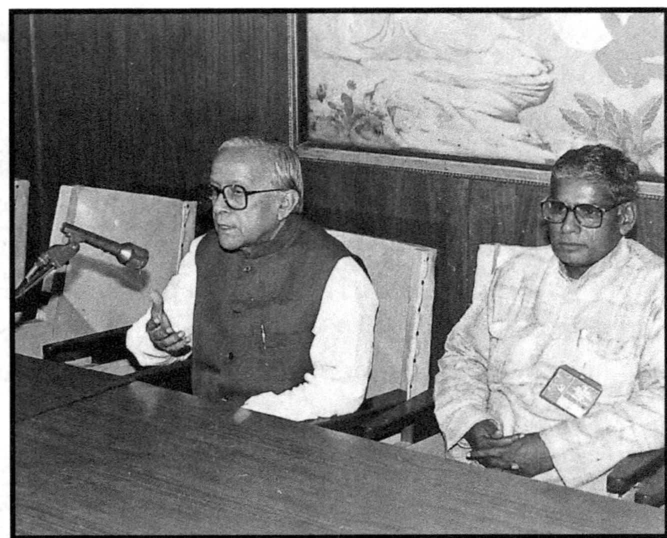

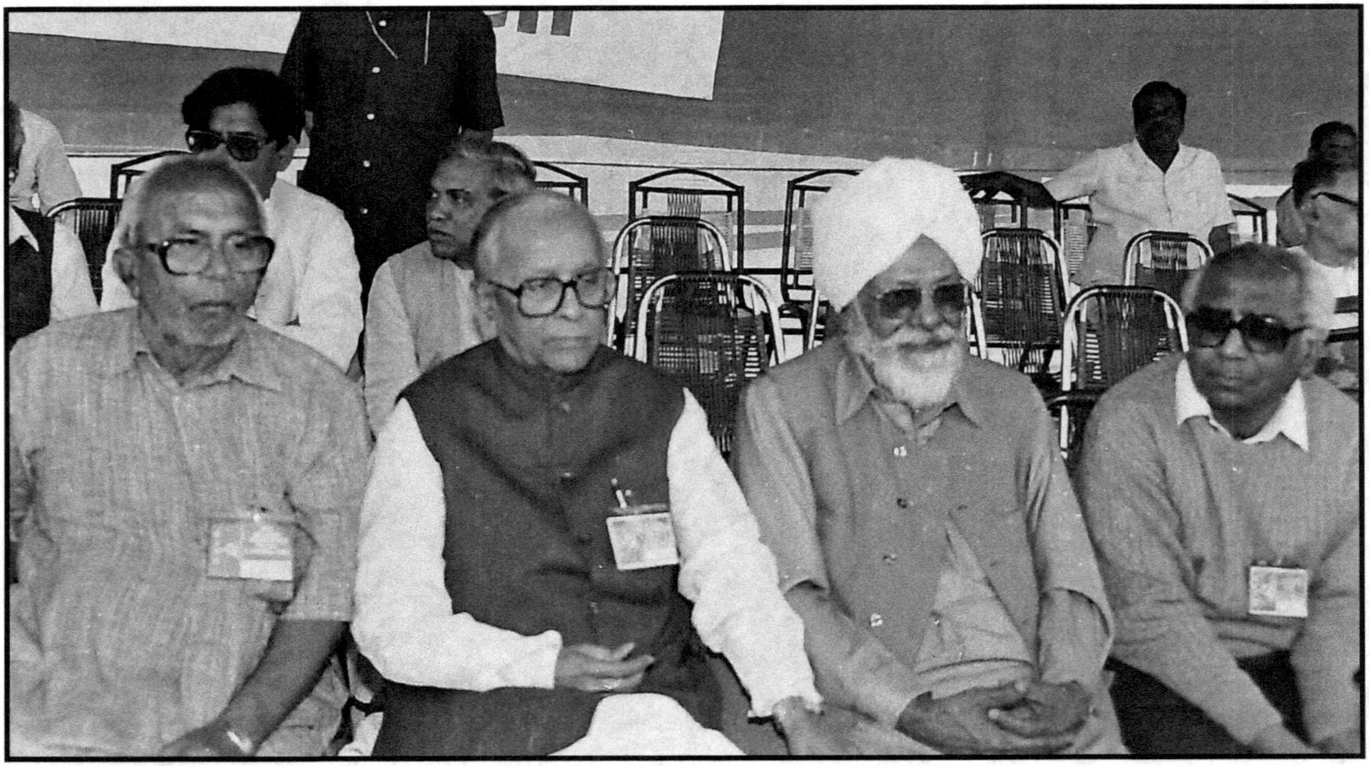

39. Kaifi Azmi and A.K. Hangal came to Patna

At the Left's rally in the 90s, famous writer Kaifi Azmi and A.K. Hangal had come to Patna. He was tired while walking, but he participated in the rally.

40. Bahujan Samaj Party in Bihar

In 1991, Patna's Gandhi Maidan, a rally was held by Kanshi Ram, the founder and national president of the Bahujan Samaj Party, alongside Mayawati. Kanshi Ram's rallies were significant events in themselves; he was vigorous and charismatic, drawing dedicated supporters from Uttar Pradesh. The rally was powerful, creating expectations of a shift in Bihar's marginalized vote towards their cause, but this did not materialize.

Pix : Rajiv

41. Ironman T.N. Seshan

T.N. Seshan was the first election commissioner to include Moral Code of Conduct. He was the in charge during tough times of election commission when polls were almost riots and there used to be lot of unrest.

Pix; Rajiv

Rajiv

42. Maneka Gandhi

The representative conference of Bihar Pradesh Sanjay Manch was held on 25 June 1985 at Babu Veer Kunwar Singh Nagar, Amrai Nawada Shahpur, Bhojpur. The conference was inaugurated by the President of the Forum, Smt. Maneka Gandhi. This was one of the biggest meetings of that time. Let it be known that this area belonged to the then Chief Minister Bindeshwari Dubey ji. Vinod Tripathi, who was in-charge of Bihar, repeatedly asked the then Bihar President Rajiv Ranjan Prasad, "Will the meeting go well, right?" Maneka ji was very happy after the conference. Many programs of Sanjay Manch took place in Bihar, in which Dharampal Singh and Ramanand Yadav were also involved. Later Ramanand Yadav became MLA and currently he is RJD's MLA from Fatuha Assembly. Shortly thereafter, Sanjay Manch merged with Janata Dal.

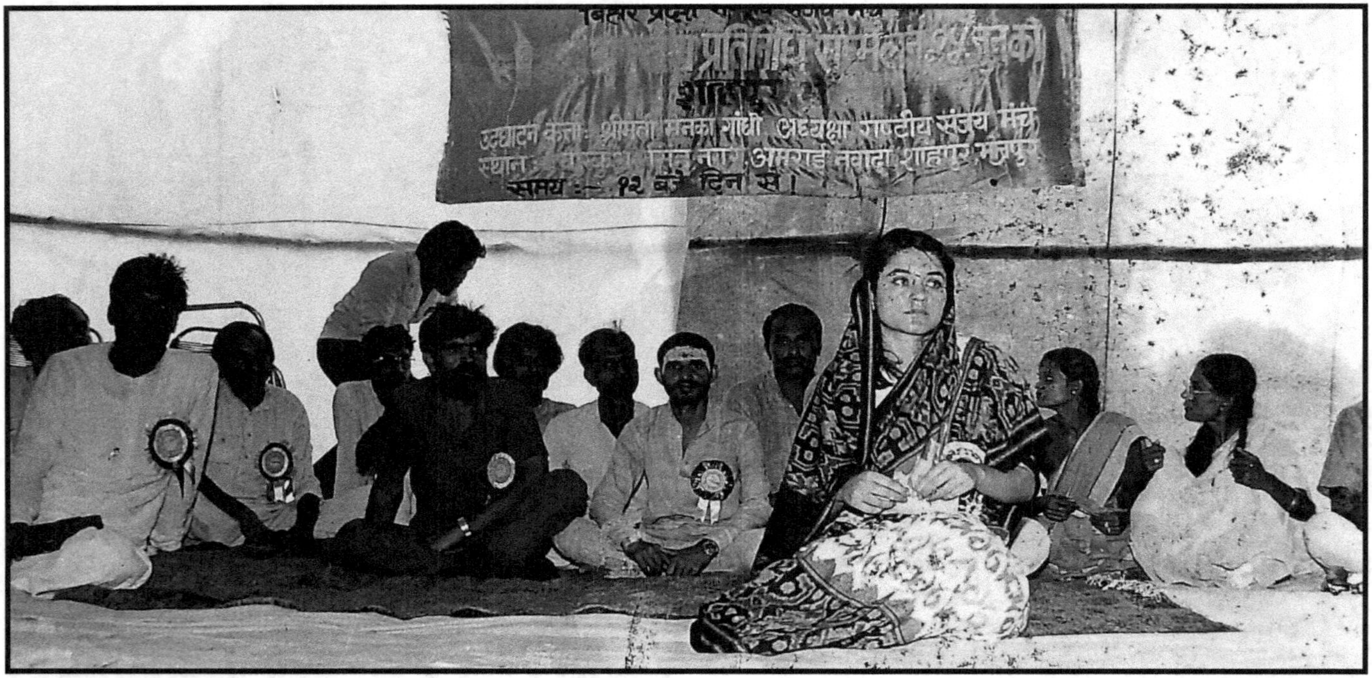
बिहार प्रदेश
गांधी अध्यक्षा राष्ट्रीय संजय मंच
समय :- १२ बजे दिन से।

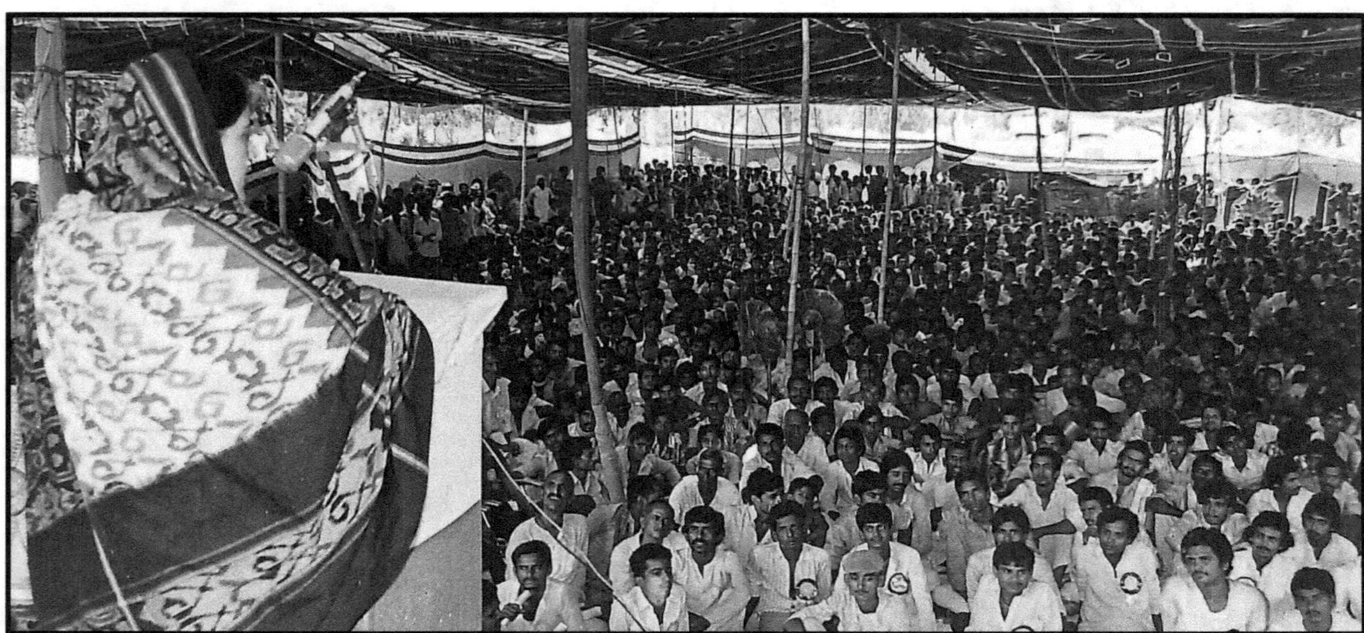

43. George Fernandes

George Mathew Fernandes was an Indian trade unionist, statesman, and journalist, who served as the 22nd Defence Minister of India from 1998 until 2004. A veteran socialist, he was a member of the Lok Sabha for over 30 years, starting from Bombay in 1967 till 2009 mostly representing constituencies from Bihar.

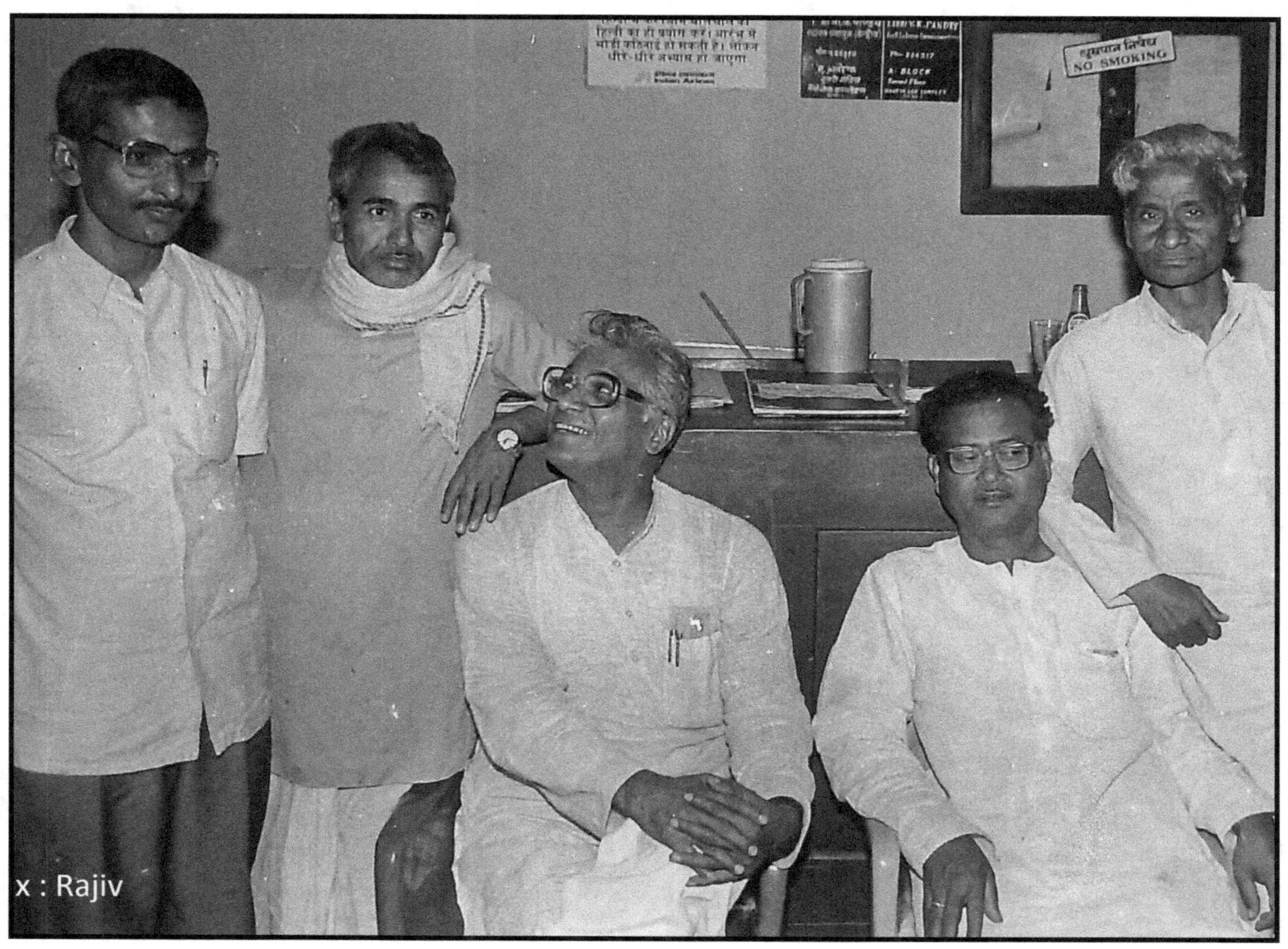

44. Chaudhary Charan Singh

The provincial meeting of Bihar Lok Dal was held on 20 August 1982 at the Memorial Hall of S.K. All the leaders of the state were present in this meeting. Chaudhary Charan Singh ji in his speech as always emphasized on how to help the farmers. In his speeches, special attention was paid to the welfare of farmers and solutions to their problems. All the prominent leaders of the state were present in the meeting, making this meeting important.

Pix : Rajiv

ix : Rajiv

लोकदल
बिहार
Pix : Raji

समता पार्टी व लोकदल
विलय सम्मेलन
Pix : Rajiv

45. President Giani Zail Singh

The then Excellency President Giani Zail Singh ji met the senior journalists of that time one by one at Patna Raj Bhavan. On this occasion, President Giani Zail Singh ji easily met all the journalists and photographers. It was a press meeting called by the public relations department, which also included bureau chiefs, news editors and photographers. This photo is of December 3, 1985.

46. Girija Prasad Koirala's visit to Patna

Hon. Girija Prasad Koirala, the Prime Minister of Nepal, visited Patna in the 1990s. According to protocol, Chief Minister Lalu Prasad Yadav welcomed him. Koirala ji unveiled his statue at JP Niwas and admired the artwork there, also offering condolences to JP. He also wrote his thoughts in the visiting register.

Pix : Rajiv

Pix ; Rajiv

Pix ; Rajiv

47. Astronaut Rakesh Sharma in Patna

In 1984, after spending eight days in space, India's two astronauts Rakesh Sharma and Ravish Malhotra returned. They were welcomed in every state of India. In Patna, the Chief Minister was Chandra Shekhar Singh. They also spoke to the press in Patna and met a significant number of political figures. Among them were District Magistrate Rajkumar Singh and SSP Kishor Kunal.

Pix : Rajiv

Pix : Rajiv

Pix : Rajiv

48. National Conference of Women's Liberation Movement

In the 1990s, discussions were underway on the subject of atrocities against women, leading to a national conference organized by the Women's Liberation Movement. The conference was held at Braj Kishor Bhavan. People from all corners of the country and abroad also attended. Due to the cold weather, most activities took place indoors, with communal meals often under shade. Various organizations were working towards the empowerment of women, aiming to educate women on how to assert their rights.

Pix : Rajiv

Pix : Rajiv

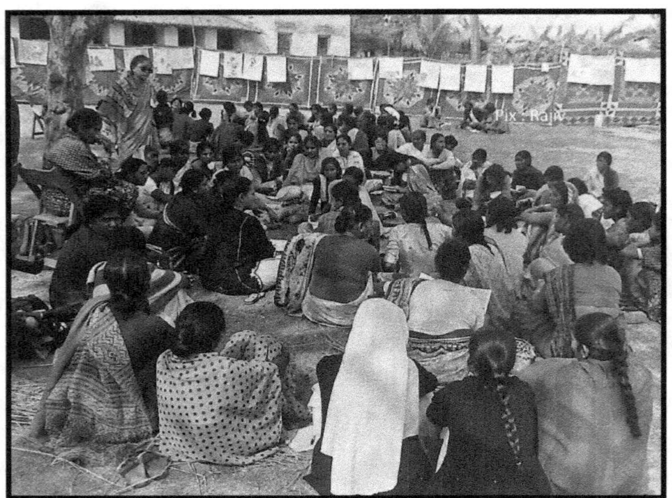

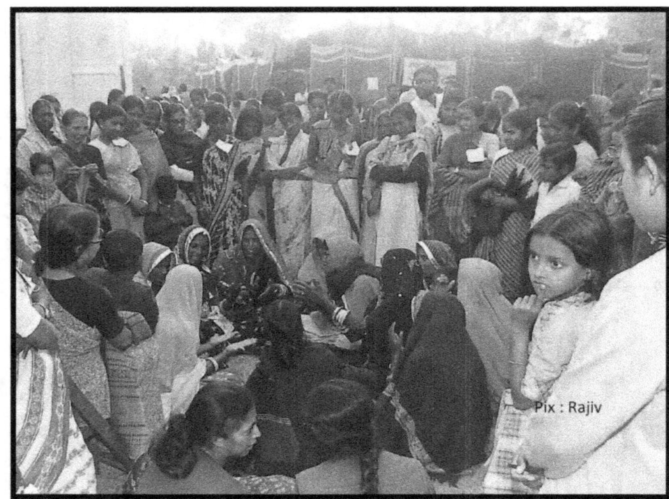

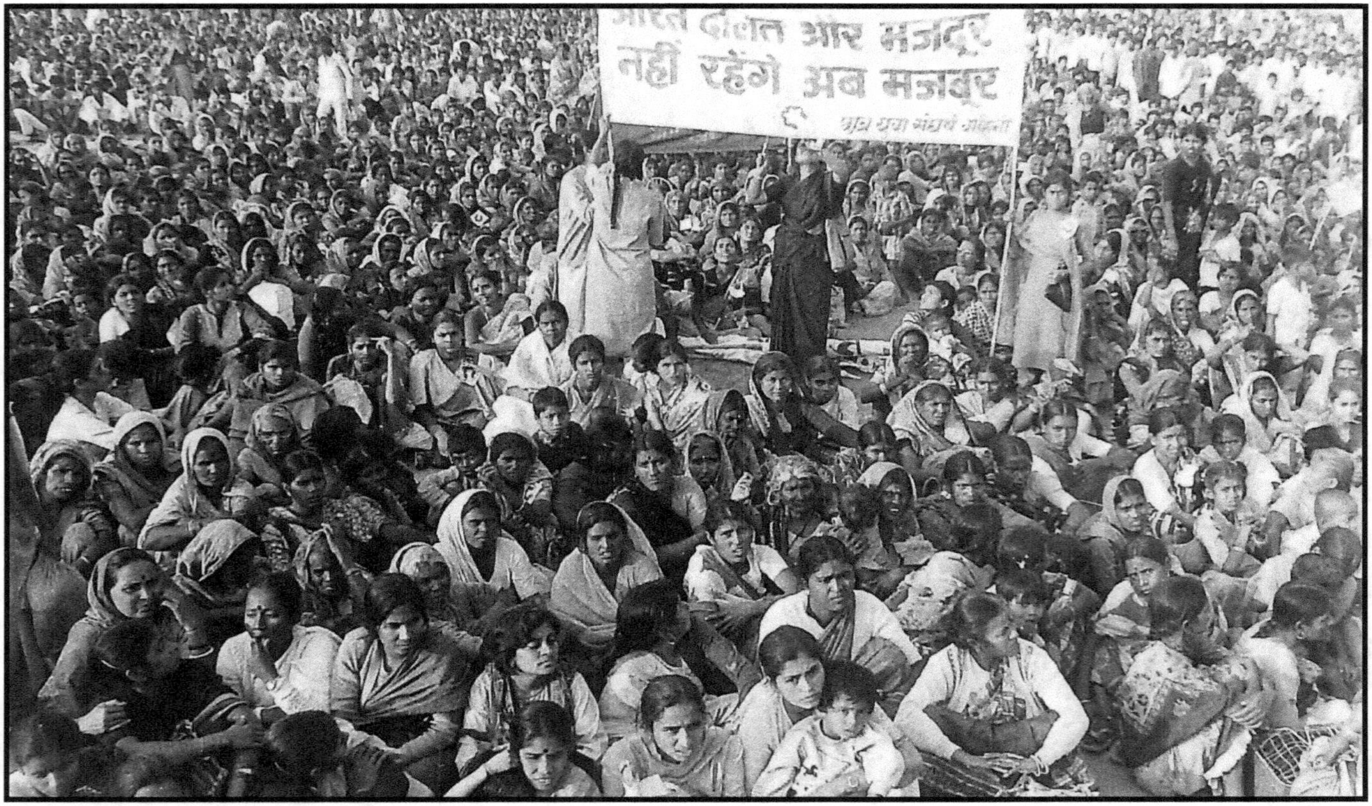
दलित और मजदूर
नहीं रहेंगे अब मजबूर

Pix : Rajiv

Pix : Rajiv

49. Vaishali Mahotsav

In 1988, Indian Vice President Shankar Dayal Sharma inaugurated the Vaishali Mahotsav in Vaishali, Bihar. The event was organized by South India Mandapam Society. The occasion included film actor Sunil Dutt, MP Vaijanti Mala, and special guests. Vaijanti Mala and Sunil Dutt were also present at the request of Kishori Sinha and LP Shahi, in the context of the film Amrapali and Vaishali.

Pix : Rajiv
OF BHARTI MANDAPAM
1988
Pix : Rajiv

Pix : Rajiv
Pix : Rajiv

Pix : Rajiv

Pix : Rajiv

50. Gayathri Pariwar Event in Patna

By Shanti Kunj Haridwar, Ashvamedha Yagya was organized by All World Gayatri Parivar at Patna on 23-02-1994. In this yagya, venerable Mata Bhagwati Devi Sharma, Pranab Pandya, Shail Didi, and Chief Minister Lalu Prasad Yadav inaugurated the yagya. Lalu ji had reached the puja mandap greeting everyone including his cabinet members Raghunath Jha, Ramchandra Purve, senior officials of Bihar government and my elder cousin WN Singh.

51. Bandhua Mukti Morcha

The first Rastriya Chaupal organized by Bandhua Mukti Morcha was held from 7 April to 9 April 1984 at Paneri Dam, Chainpur, Daltenganj. Mahasweta Devi and Swami Agnivesh ji were the chief guests in this event. The coordinator of the program was Rameshwaram and Suresh Bhatt was also involved in the event.

बंधुआ मुक्ति मोर्चा द्वारा आयोजित
राष्ट्रीय चौपाल

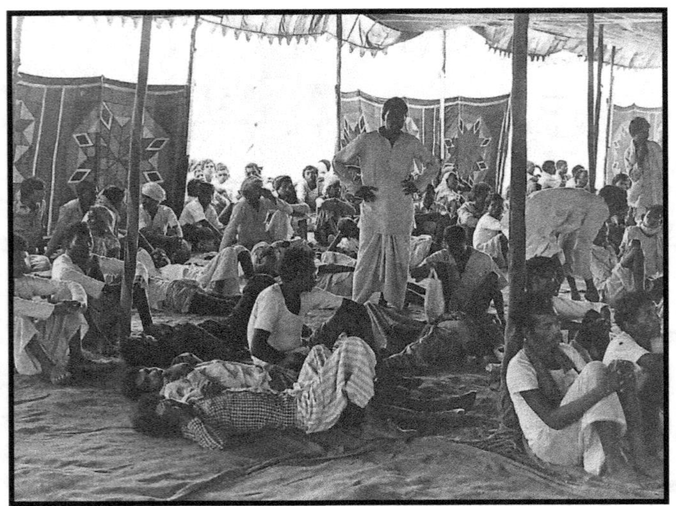

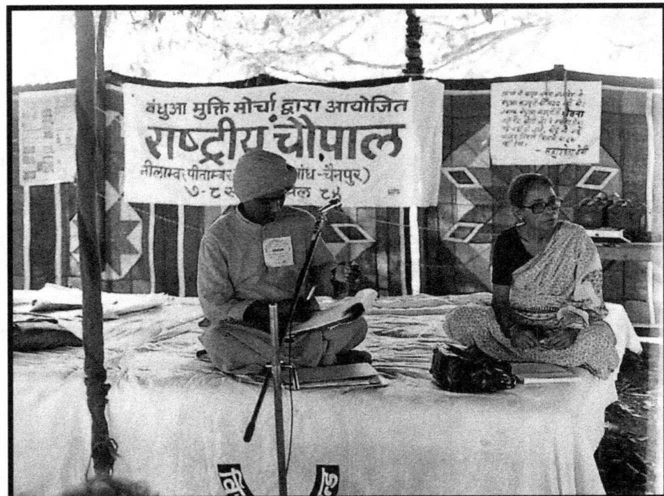

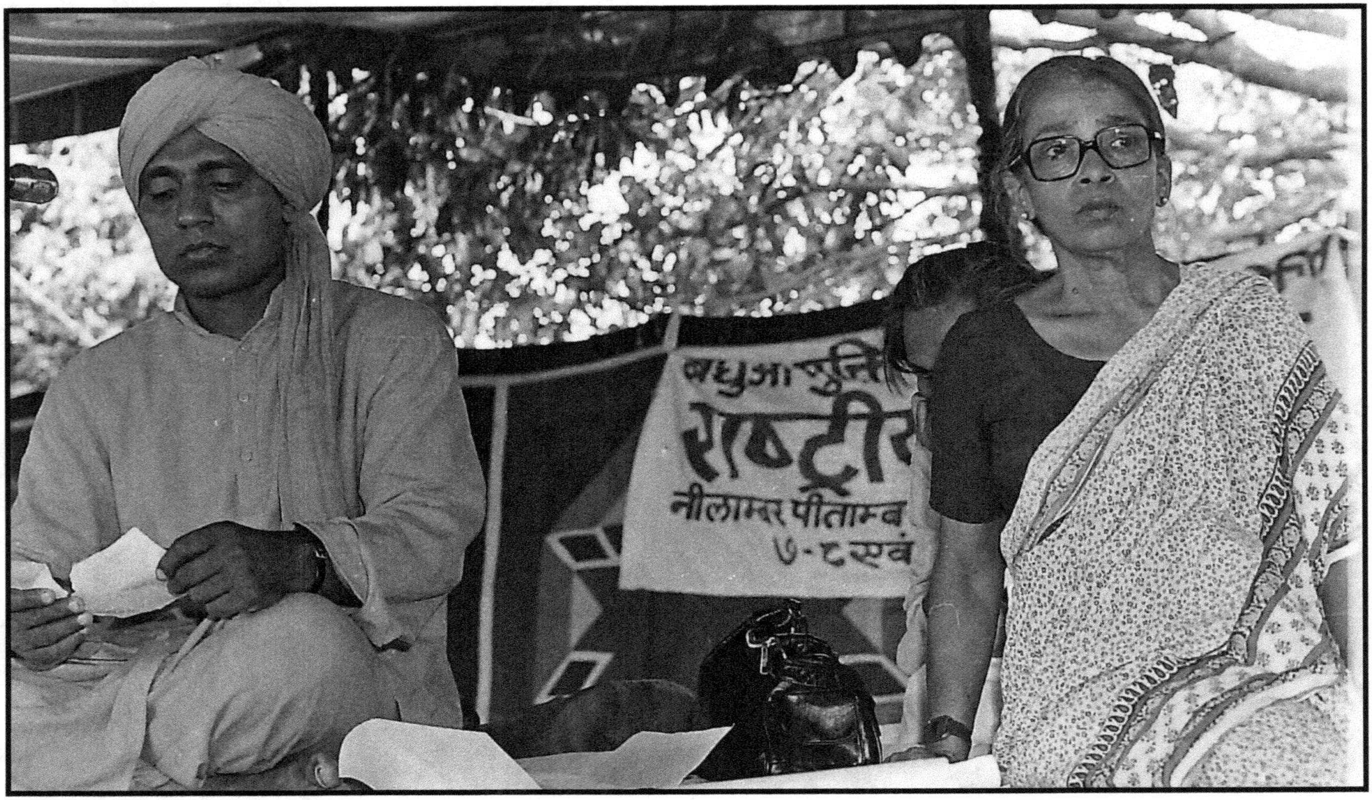

During this conference, 12 bonded labourers were freed. This was perhaps the first instance when such liberation took place during a ceremony. Later, bonded labourers were freed in Mirzapur and other places also. This event proved to be an important step against bonded labour and inspired many other efforts in this direction.

52. Magahi Poet Mathura Prasad Navin ji

This is about the days of Navbharat Times when the local editor was Arun Ranjan. In a meeting, Arun Ranjan decided to start a special column written by writers, journalists, artists, and such people to help them. During this time, Navendu and I went to Magahi in Bihar to meet poet Mathura Prasad Navin. He was not at home, so we asked some people to find him. His wife, Ganga Ji, was bathing. After a while, Navin arrived and we began discussing. Among his famous poems is "Ramdhani Tohar Beta Bot Mein Bahak Gelo." After a lot of discussion, we convinced him to write a column for Navbharat Times and returned. While pasting pages at night, Navendu read Navin's poem in his own style before pasting the page. The next day, there was much discussion about Navin's poem and article in the newspaper.

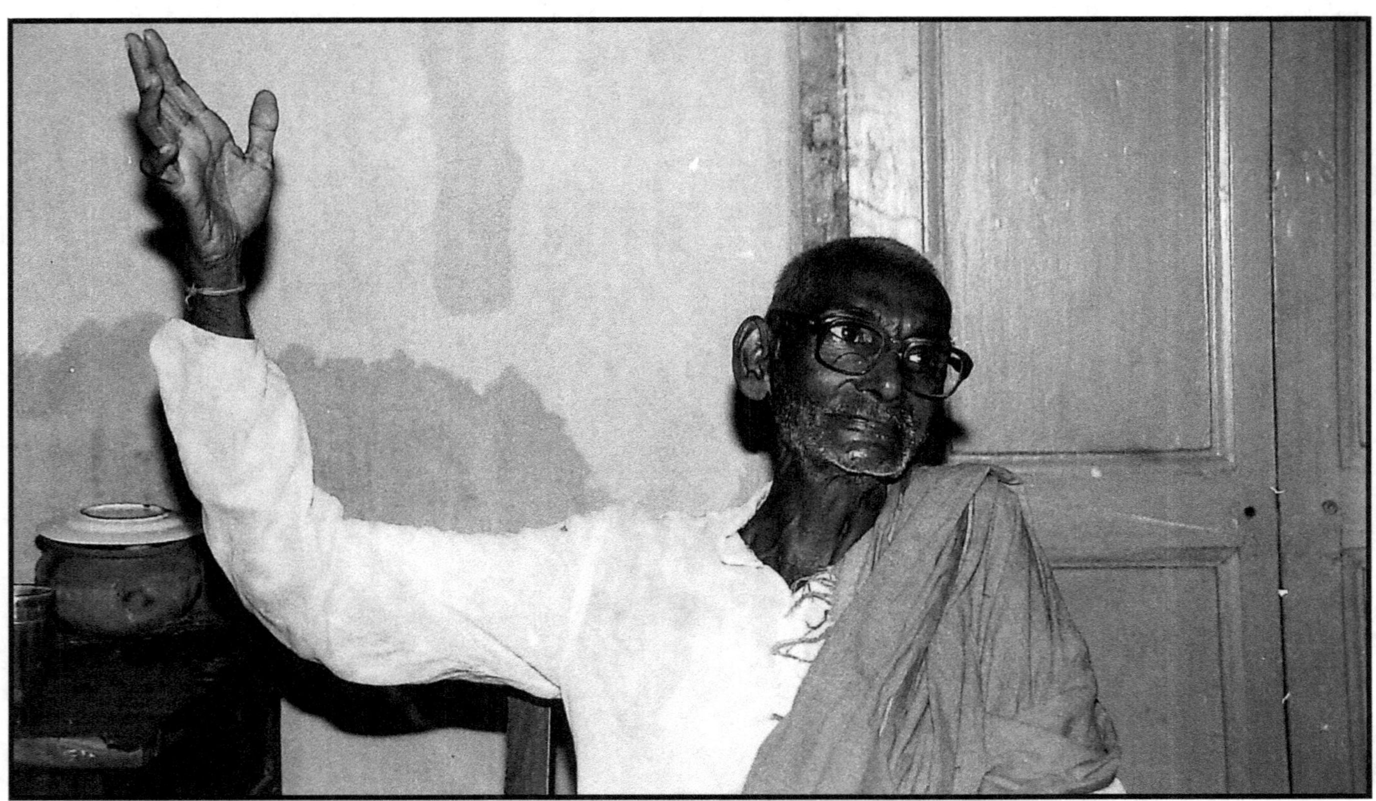

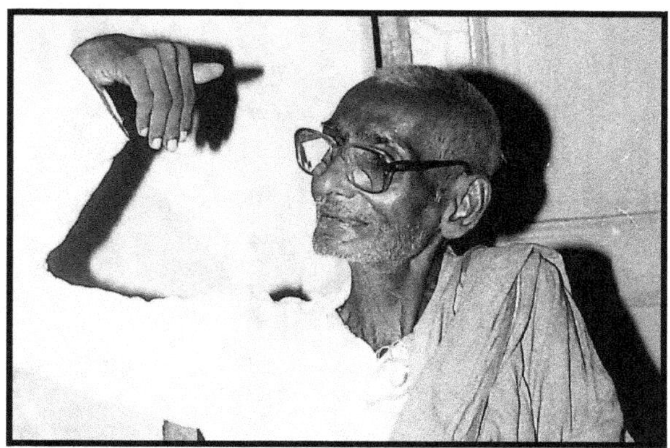

53. Meeting Milkha Singh

This is a story from the 1980s. Badri Prasad Yadav used to do sports commentary, write stories, and present programs for All India Radio Patna. He had also represented Bihar at the national level in football. I, along with Badri Prasad Yadav, and the great sprinter Milkha Singh visited Patna. We scheduled an interview with Milkha Singh, which Badri and I conducted together. The interview lasted for half an hour. Badri began with: "This is All India Radio Patna, and now you will hear a special interview with Milkha Singh by Badri Prasad Yadav," and then the conversation started. The discussion was quite thrilling. Milkha Singh shared how he used to practice in his time despite the lack of resources, driven by his determination to achieve his goals.

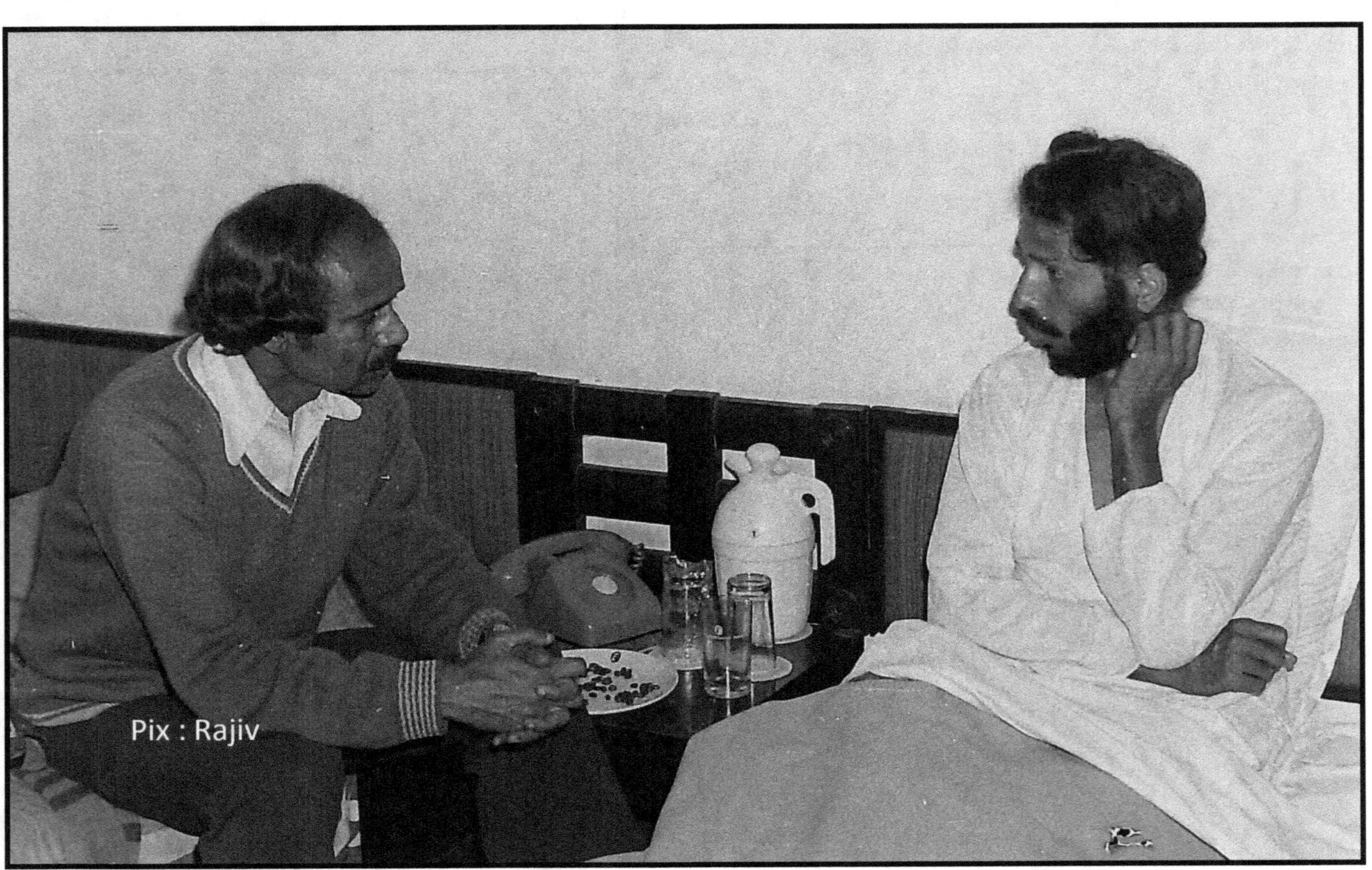

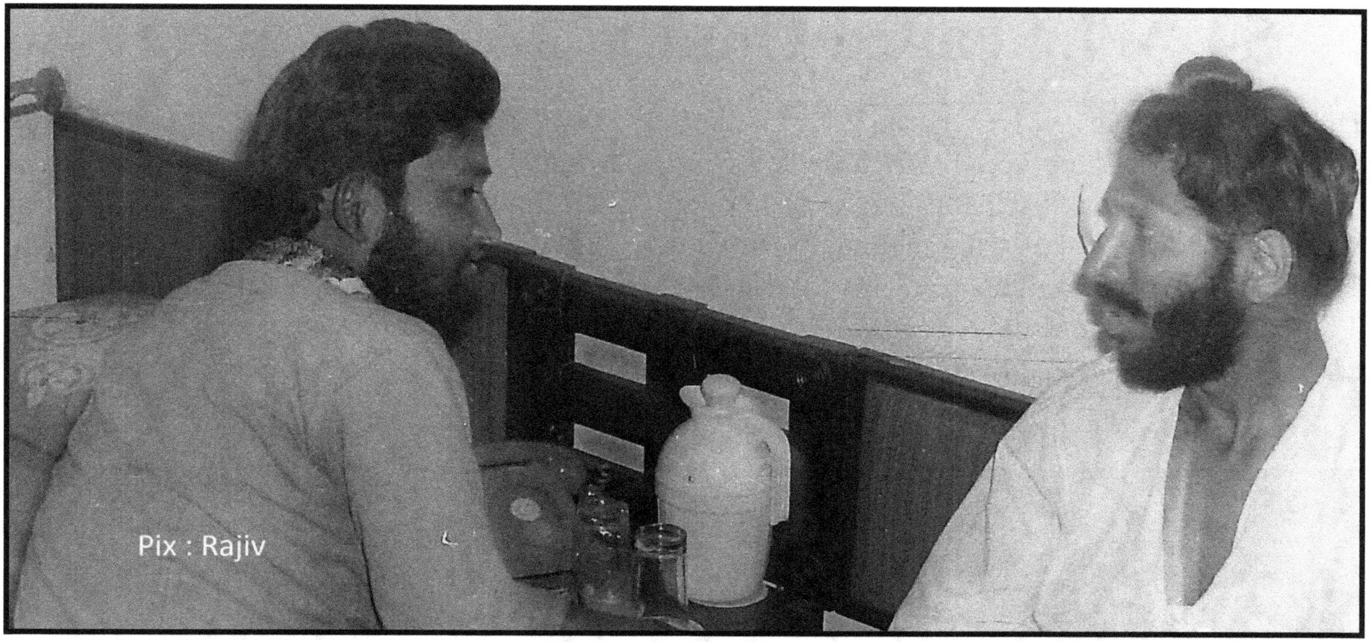

Pix : Rajiv

Pix : Rajiv

54. Who called Gandhi Ji a Mahatma?

This is a story from 1981. According to the diary of Pandit Rajkumar Shukla, when Gandhi was returning to India from South Africa, Pandit Rajkumar Shukla went to Mumbai port to welcome him. As Gandhi was disembarking from the ship, Shukla saw him and exclaimed, "This is the Mahatma. He can free us from the indigo cultivation." The term 'Mahatma Gandhi' is used in his diary, written in the Kaithi script. My cousin, Jugal Kishore Prasad, who actively participated in the freedom movement and was a lawyer in Samastipur, read it and told me that Rajkumar Shukla was the first person to call Gandhi 'Mahatma.'

I heard from Rajkumar Shukla's associate, Gulab Chandra Gulali, that at the Lucknow Conference, Gandhi had asked Shukla to come to Calcutta to avoid him. Shukla believed that only Mahatma Gandhi could free them from the indigo cultivation imposed by the British. Pandit Rajkumar Shukla brought Gandhi to Patna, and all these details, including the ticket number, are recorded in his diary. Shukla wrote in his diary almost daily.

अक्टूबर १५,१९५६

आश्विन २३,१८८१(

प्रिय श्री विन्ध्याचल बाबू,

मुझे यह जानकर खुशी हुई कि स्वर्गीय श्री राजकुमार शुक्ल की स्मृति में आपने "चम्पारण और नील के धब्बे" नामक पुस्तक लिखी है। पुस्तक की एक प्रति मुझे भी देखने को मिली। चम्पारण सत्याग्रह हमारे राष्ट्रीय आन्दोलन में महत्वपूर्ण स्थान रखता है और श्री राजकुमार शुक्ल उन व्यक्तियों में थे जिन्होंने उस सत्याग्रह में प्रमुख भाग लिया। मुझे उनके काफी निकट आने का अवसर मिला था और इसलिये मुझे यह पुस्तक देखकर बड़ी खुशी हुई कि इस प्रकार से उनकी स्मृति सदा ताजा रहेगी। मैं आपके इस प्रयास को स्तुत्य समझता हूं और आपको बधाई देता हूं।

आपका,

...गुप्त,

Anil Prashant and I were perhaps the first journalists to go to Chanpatia and cover Rajkumar Ji's diary and photos from his village. I heard many stories of the movement from Gulali Ji. When I went to Chanpatia, I met the local MLA, Veerval Sharma, and took photos with the people of his village. In Yogendra Shukla's village, Malkhachak, the revolutionaries used to hide. There, food and shelter were provided for everyone. While going to the restroom, they would sit and make five to ten bombs. These people were part of the extremist faction. All these things used to happen in front of Vindhyachal Prasad Gupta, also known as Kavi Ji. I stayed for three days with Anil Prashant. Kavi Ji gave us the diary on the condition that no photocopies should be made, as it is the heritage of Rajkumar Shukla and the nation. We prepared the report and submitted it to our senior writer Bhupendra Abodh Ji. I also visited Malkhachak with Abodh Ji, where Yogendra Shukla's house was. He had made significant contributions to the freedom movement. The report was rewritten and published in Maya Manohar Kahanian and Prov, but unfortunately, our names were not mentioned, which was a bit disappointing, but oh well.

55. Kalchakra in Bodh Gaya

In the first week of October 1984, the Kalchakra Bodh Gaya was observed. I had the experience that I could not find an empty place in the city. No hotel was vacant either. Thanks to Ramesh Upadhyay Ji and D.I.G. I got a room in Magadh University. There was talk about starting the program. After meeting with the P.R.O., he asked me for a photo, which I cut out from a postcard and passed on. Today I am proud to say that in the close circuit with India, Upadhyay Ji and I presented "Frontline Hindu," and Raghuray and three foreigners also participated. At that time, Raghuray did 16 pages for India Today, and I reported 13 pages in the November 1984 Frontline. Nearly ten thousand foreign correspondents and about four lakh devotees from India and abroad attended the event.

DAIJOKYO BUDDHIST TEMPLE
(JAPAN)

56. Dalai Lama

In the 1990s, the Dalai Lama, the spiritual leader of Buddhism, attended a program organized by the Charkha Committee at JP Nivas. He presented a garland to the statue of JP. Senior leader Devendra Prasad Singh, all members of the Women's Charkha Committee, and Jaynarayan Sahay also accompanied the Dalai Lama to tour the JP Memorial Room, sitting, and all other places. Later, keeping his thoughts, the Dalai Lama asked about Sudhanshu Ranjan while getting off from Patna Doordarshan.

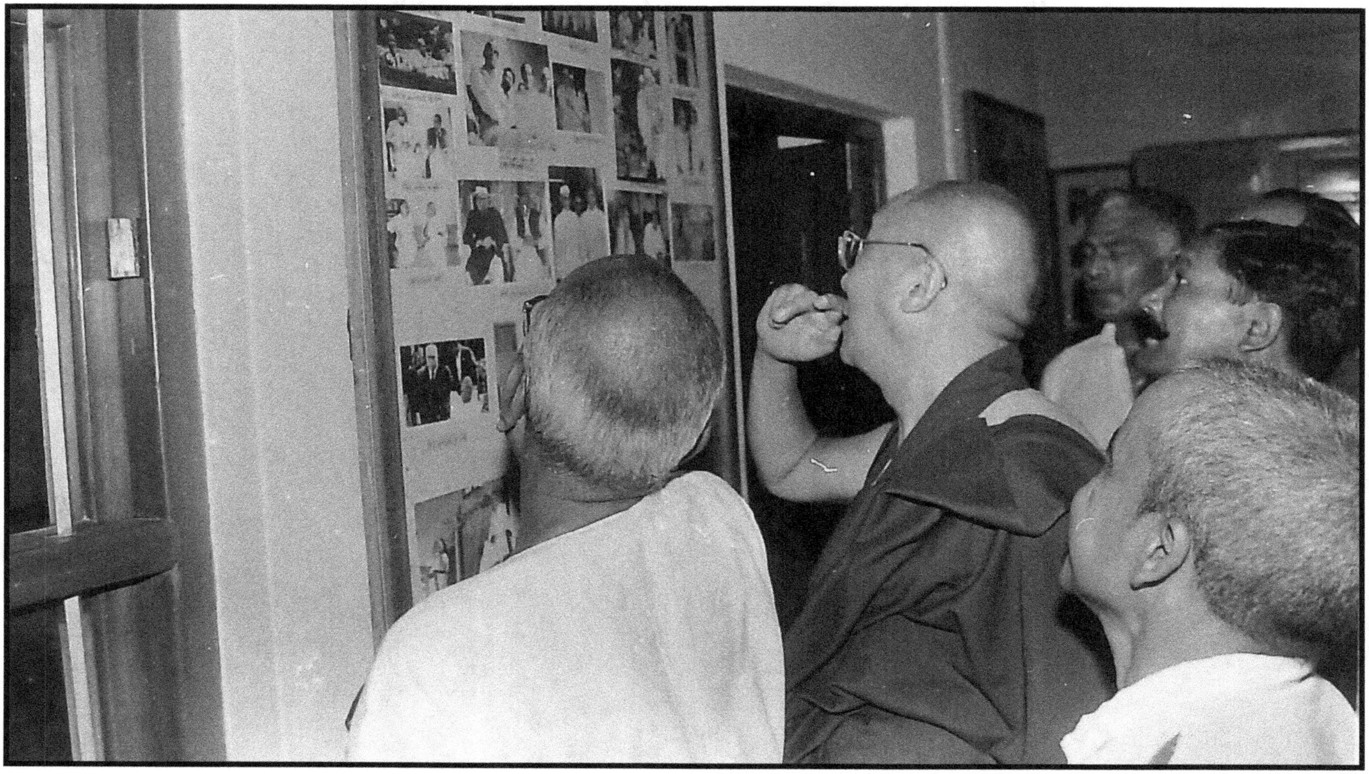

Pix : Rajiv

: Rajiv

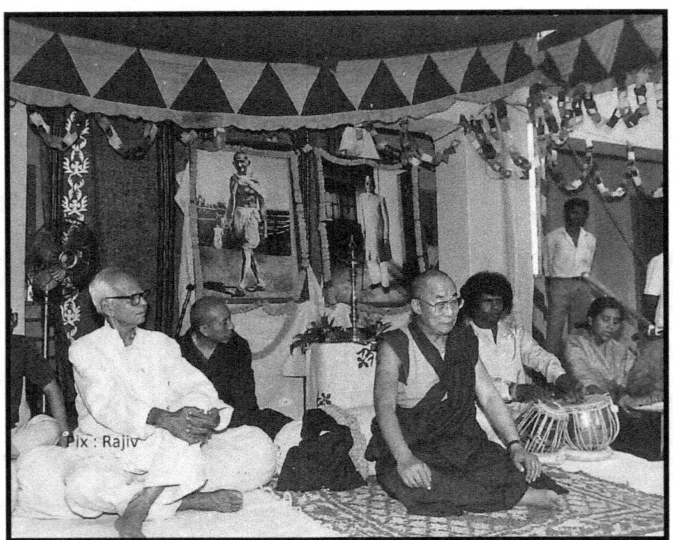

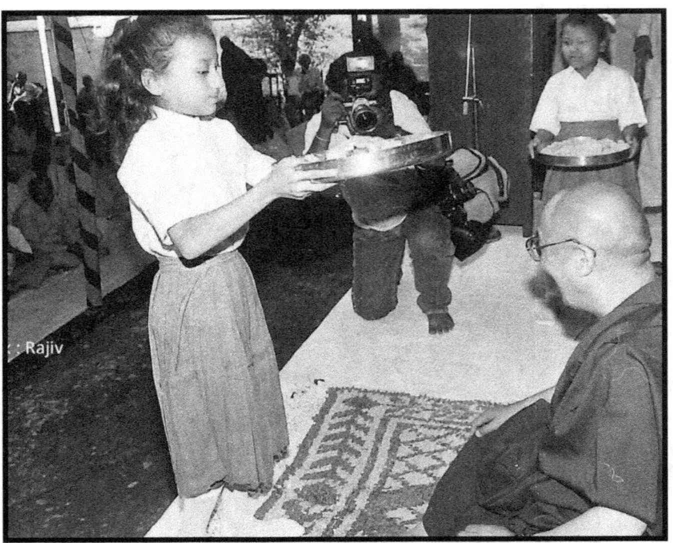

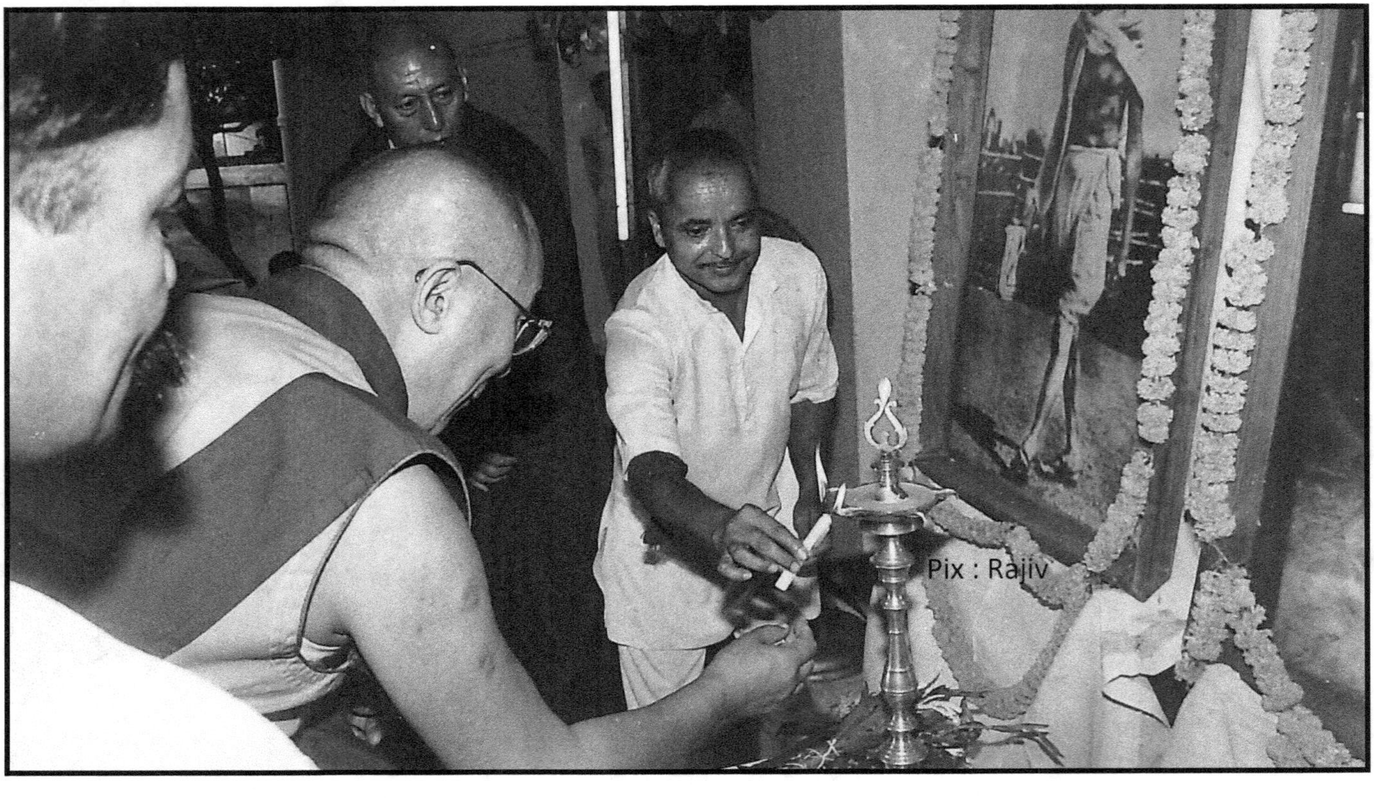
Pix : Rajiv

57. Baby Lama

It was February 1987, when a small boy from Tibet, Baby Ozel Lama, was being discussed in Bodh Gaya. It was being told that this child is a younger version of Shri Dalai Lama. This news attracted a lot of attention. I also wanted to see Baby Lama and cover his story, so I reached Bodh Gaya.

A heartfelt gratitude to Shri Shatrughan Sinha Ji, whom my father always regarded as an elder brother

We all miss you Papa

IndiePress

The best route your story can take.

To publish your own book, contact us.

We publish poetry collections, short story collections, novellas and novels.

contact@http://indiepress.in/

Instagram- indie_press